Cigarettes

Cigarettes

Anatomy of an Industry from Seed to Smoke

Tara Parker-Pope

THE NEW PRESS, NEW YORK

Published in the United States by The New Press, New York, 2001
Paperback edition, 2002
Distributed by W. W. Norton & Company, Inc., New York

LIBRARY OF CONGRESS CATALOGING-IN-PUBLICATION DATA
Parker-Pope, Tara.
Cigarettes: anatomy of an industry from seed to smoke / Tara Parker-Pope.
p. cm.
Includes index.
ISBN 1-56584-503-X (hc.)
ISBN 1-56584-743-1 (pbk.)
1. Cigarette industry—History. 2. Cigarette industry—United States—History.
3. Tobacco industry—History. 4. Tobacco industry—United States—History.
5. Cigarette—habit—Social aspects. 6. Cigarette habit—Health aspects. I. Title.
HD9149.C42P372001
338.4'767973'09733—dc21   00–040181

The New Press was established in 1990 as a not-for-profit alternative to the
large, commercial publishing houses currently dominating the book publishing
industry. The New Press operates in the public interest rather than for private
gain, and is committed to publishing, in innovative ways, works of educational,
cultural, and community value that are often deemed insufficiently profitable.

The New Press, 450 West 41st Street, 6th floor, New York, NY 10036
www.thenewpress.com

Book design by Ellen Cipriano

Printed in the United States of America

2 4 6 8 10 9 7 5 3 1

Contents

Preface

I smoked my first cigarette back in the middle of the Reagan years—a Benson & Hedges Menthol Light that I lit up during a late-night chat in the halls of a University of Texas dorm room. My initiation into the world of smokers came courtesy of my roommate, who regularly invited me to keep her company on her "smoke breaks," which she took just outside the door of our tiny room. Smoking, after all, is a social ritual, and smokers enjoy sharing the habit. My already-slender roommate had started smoking a few years earlier in a bid to stay that way—the same reason millions of other women say led them to start smoking.

Although we'd taken dozens of smoking breaks from our studies together that year, I'd so far skipped out on the smoking part of the respite. But on this particular occasion, for reasons I can't remember now, she hesitated before lighting her cigarette.

"Want one?" she said. She picked up the blue-silver pack and tilted it my way, a movement that, as it happened, lifted a cigarette just slightly, but enticingly, out of the package.

This, in the vernacular of the consumer products industry,

was a "trial decision"—that pivotal moment on the continuum of consumer behavior when years of Hollywood images, event sponsorship, and billions of dollars worth of hip, aspirational advertising pounds at the subconscious mind of a new consumer. By cigarette industry standards, I was a late bloomer. A 19-year-old is far from a sure thing in the tobacco business—75 percent of lifetime smokers start by age 17. More than 90 percent of smokers who wait until after the ripe old age of 21 to start smoking quickly drop the habit completely[1]

Also working in my favor was the fact that I was raised in a family of nonsmokers. We even had little "Thank you for not smoking" stickers pasted in the ashtrays of our car. Sociologists would say the prohibition against smoking in my house might have tilted me toward the smokers' camp—the allure of forbidden fruit, they say—though my family's antismoking fervor had managed to protect me from tobacco's seduction for the first 19 years of my life.

But not from the message. As a child, an affinity for camels, the animal, prompted me to collect Camels, the brand: packs of cigarettes, advertisements, and even posters of the now-retired "Old Joe" cartoon camel (which R. J. Reynolds insists didn't appeal to children). In high school, the budding feminist in me regularly clipped ads featuring those beautiful, career-minded Virginia Slims smokers, who reminded me what a long, long way women had come. (Little did I know that women had come so far that they were now smoking and dying of smoking-related illnesses at the same rate as men.)

By 1985, I may not have been a smoker, but I was amply prepared to become one. There I was outside my dorm room, smack in the middle of my own personal trial decision, eyeing that slender Benson & Hedges Menthol Light, on the cusp of joining the ranks of the 50 million Americans who smoke cigarettes. The tobacco industry was spending an estimated $4 billion annually to advertise and promote its brands in the United States.[2] At the movies, Demi Moore and the rest of the brat pack were puffing away in *St. Elmo's Fire*, and they looked damn good doing it. So did my roommate.

Of course I took the cigarette.

It wouldn't be my last. Smoking turned out to be a decidedly handy habit to have, keeping me awake through college all-nighters and helping to calm me during times of crisis. My cigarette was well-suited to angst-ridden, philosophical talks at the Captain Quackenbush coffee bar. My ideas on existentialism seemed so much deeper and persuasive when they were interrupted by a long, slow drag. (Sartre, after all, was a smoker.) Later, the cigarette served as a handy prop during my days as a student reporter at the college newspaper. It was only the stifling Austin heat that kept me from donning a trench coat and completing the look.

Ah, but here's where my personal tobacco journey ends. Life after college isn't so easy for smokers. My first newsroom was disappointingly antiseptic. Smokers were initially relegated to a separate smoking area and were later exiled outside. (So much for my romanticized view of the smoking hack.) I continued as an occasional smoker for a couple of years, but for reasons science can't explain, I didn't get hooked. Eventually, without even realizing it, I had stopped smoking. I don't even remember my last cigarette.

Most smokers aren't so lucky. Only 10 percent of smokers can take it or leave it. That means 90 percent of the people who use cigarettes are addicts.[3] It is a captive market that needs little maintenance. No other product—or at least nothing sold legally—has that kind of hold on its user. (By comparison, only about 10 percent of the people who drink alcohol, another popular drug, develop a compulsion to drink.) In short, keeping smokers smoking is relatively easy given that, for most of them, addiction is a fundamental component of the habit. It's getting them to start that's the challenge.

And that is why that first trial decision is so pivotal to the future of the tobacco industry. The business of cigarettes is geared entirely to that moment of truth when another consumer might join the fraternity of smokers. From the plants the industry chooses to grow, to the methods they use to blend the leaves and carefully control a cigarette's nicotine content and the packaging, to the distribution and advertising of a pack of cigarettes, the goal of tobacco companies is to keep current customers hooked and to attract new smokers. The marketing of cigarettes has been boiled down to a science that outsiders, with the help of newly released internal industry documents, are now only beginning to understand. It was no less than a student of Freud, Edward Bernays, who put smoking on the couch, dissecting smokers' minds and handing cigarette advertisers the potent messages that launched a generation of women smokers and continue to attract smokers today. Dozens of cigarette brands ensure that there is a smoke for everyone and every taste and every image. If you are under the age of 21 or female or a minority or are a native of Asia or eastern Europe, you are in the sights of the tobacco industry.

But how did an ugly brown plant—poisonous even to those who pick its leaves—turn into one of the world's most profitable businesses churning out $300 billion[4] in sales annually? The story of the cigarette's journey begins more than 500 years ago with the discovery of tobacco, a strange "Indian vice" that even its earliest users recognized as addictive—and lucrative. But it was the invention in the late 1880s of the modern cigarette—crushed tobacco leaves rolled up in paper by a machine—that transformed the tobacco industry. Because the cigarette, unlike pipe tobacco or snuff, was actually manufactured, cigarette makers could charge a premium for the smoke, even though it was still relatively cheap to make. And simply by virtue of its design, the cigarette is more addictive than other forms of tobacco, an intrinsic difference that fueled a steep increase in consumption during the twentieth century and helped build cigarette powerhouses like Philip Morris Cos., R.J. Reynolds Tobacco, and British-American Tobacco Company. Those companies, in turn, helped drive cigarette consumption by launching a new era of marketing and branding linking cigarettes with sophistication, self-confidence, and freedom. Today, those same firms control much of the world's cigarette production.

But surely, haven't health worries and a slew of antitobacco laws and litigation quelled the cigarette juggernaut? To be sure, in many developed countries where consumers have been inundated with the antitobacco health message, cigarette consumption has dropped during the past few decades. But despite the popular image of big tobacco on the ropes (remember the unseemly moment when U.S. tobacco executives promised to tell the truth before Congress?), a closer look at the industry shows that even in the wake of a $246 billion settlement with all 50 U.S. states, little has really changed for the industry. Despite an increasingly hostile regulatory climate, billions of dollars in litigation and settlement costs, and stacks of documents that have recently unveiled some of the industry's most closely guarded secrets, the cigarette business remains a highly profitable growth industry.

The reason for the seeming paradox is simple: Manufacturers' skyrocketing legal bills simply have been passed on to smokers, who are willing to pay the price. And even as smoking rates in big markets like the United States and Europe flatten out, those regions are still the most profitable for cigarette makers—after all, about a quarter of the population in the United States and Europe still smoke, and new, younger smokers are joining their ranks every day. In addition, cigarette makers have moved into new lucrative markets such as Russia, eastern Europe, and Asia, where the regulation of cigarette marketing is often lax and where cigarette users, perhaps because of larger issues like rising food costs, unemployment, and political unrest, have shown little concern about the health consequences of smoking.

When I first began writing tobacco stories in 1995, I did so with a grudging admiration for Big Tobacco. My sense was that whether or not one believes the tobacco companies are engaged in a morally dubious trade, tobacco, as an enterprise, is a remarkable success story. I still believe that. Nonetheless, it's impossible to engage in a discussion of cigarettes as a business without considering their enormous human cost. Cigarettes are a deadly product, so deadly that Surgeon General C. Everett Koop, one of Big Tobacco's most vigilant opponents, likes to conjure the image of three fully booked jumbo jets crashing to the earth every day for an entire year to represent the number of people who die each year from tobacco-related illnesses in the United States alone. Is there any other consumer product that, when used according to manufacturers' instructions, could result in the death of its user?

The story of tobacco as a business is a remarkable one, not in spite of the health consequences of cigarettes but *because* of them. Most smokers smoke with the full knowledge that each cigarette will shorten each of their lives by seven minutes and may ultimately cause a slow, painful death. Even so, regular smokers spend tens of thousands of dollars over a lifetime on the habit. They are ostracized from the office, restaurants, and friends' homes, and they suffer through airplane rides, church services, and childrens' recitals, thinking the entire time about the next opportunity to dash out for a cigarette. The acrid odor of cigarettes makes smokers smell bad and dulls their senses of smell and taste. Their fingers turn yellow and their teeth turn brown. Still, most continue to smoke.

This book is by no means a definitive account of the tobacco industry. It is, instead, a sort of primer on a business that is, for better and worse, a paragon of the capitalistic ideal. Cigarettes are a savvy, highly profitable industry that continues to give more than 1.1 billion people around the world what they want in spite of relentless pressure from opponents to stop. How the cigarette makers do it, from the moment they plant the tobacco seeds to that crucial consumer trial decision, is the story I've tried to tell here.

My tenure as a smoker lasted a little over four years. But they were memorable years. Even now, sitting at my desk or staying up late at night working at the computer, I still hold a pen between my index and third fingers, suck in, and slowly exhale.

List of Figures

List of Illustrations

1.

Lighting Up:
A Brief History of the Cigarette

*"A cigarette is the perfect type of a perfect pleasure. It is exquisite,
and it leaves one unsatisfied. What more can one want?"*
—OSCAR WILDE

A Smoky New World

The cigarette is the only manufactured product found in almost
every corner of the world, and it is recognized—if not used—by virtually every human being on the planet. Certainly no other product
is as ubiquitous. Cereal? Razor blades? Chewing gum? Not even
Coca-Cola has the global reach of the cigarette. "It's a wonderful
product," says Gary Black, a longtime Wall Street tobacco analyst
and a former smoker. "If you give someone a cigarette in the most
backwards country in the world, they will know what to do with it."

The world's tobacco companies produce an estimated 5.5 tril-
lion cigarettes each year. That's nearly one thousand cigarettes for
every person on the planet, as though every child has received an
allotment of fifty packs a year at birth. More than 15 billion cigarettes are sold each day to more than 1.1 billion people puffing
away around the world.[1] How did such an eminently simple prod-

uct—a bunch of crushed leaves wrapped in paper—become such big business?

Today's smokers have no less than Christopher Columbus to thank for introducing them to the pleasures and hazards of smoking. A South American native in a canoe reportedly gave Columbus some tobacco leaves when he first landed in the New World in 1492. Later, explorers spotted the natives smoking from a Y-shaped contraption called a *tobaca*. It was an early version of the pipe, guaranteed to give users a concentrated hit. The two prongs were put into the nostrils while the end of the pipe was set in burning tobacco leaves. Centuries before modern scientists would debate the addictive nature of tobacco, Columbus had it figured out. Watching his sailors puff away the hours, he noted that "it was not within their power to refrain" from it. Columbus's men took the new plant back to Europe, where for the next 50 years it was a smelly vice of sailors and a curiosity cultivated by botanists.

But as has often proved the case in the history and business of tobacco, all the plant needed was a little marketing. That came in the guise of French ambassador Jean Nicot and English explorer Sir Walter Raleigh. Nicot was a French ambassador to Portugal when he learned of a man who claimed tobacco had cured his chronic skin ulcer. Nicot was soon convinced of the powers of this "Indian herb of marvelous and proved worth against [ailments] given up as incurable by the physicians." In 1560 he sent some tobacco seeds to Catherine de Medici, the queen mother of France, with descriptions of the herb's curative powers. Word spread, and tobacco gained a reputation across Europe as a wonder drug. The plant, whose botanical name is genus *Nicotiana* in honor of its biggest promoter, launched a new era in medicine. Medical books espoused the curative powers of tobacco for everything from flatulence to rabies, as an antiseptic, and as a cure for headaches. Pity the poor asthmatics of the time—doctors recommended tobacco smoke as the cure. For pearly whites, rub teeth with tobacco ashes. A bad memory? Sixteenth-century physicians

ELEGANT PREVENTIVE OF THE CHOLERA.

Cheroots of a mild a flavor, as to be smoked by the most delicate females, are imported by Puff & Cᵒ. They are recommended to the attention of Ladies as the most effectual preventive of Cholera.

see Tobacconist's Advertisement.

Women Smoking to Prevent Cholera
(courtesy of New York Public Library)

suggested tobacco smoke because it "rose to the brain, the seat of recollection." The plague? Smoking, the medical establishment believed, would keep it at bay, prompting widespread smoking during the Great Plague of 1665. During the plague years, boys at England's Eton College were whipped if they tried to skip their daily smoke.

But if smokers have a patron saint, it is Sir Walter Raleigh, credited as the first to promote smoking for pleasure. Raleigh, a swashbuckling explorer and a favorite of the queen of England, was something of a trendsetter in the fashion-conscious circles of Elizabethan London. And he loved to smoke, picking up the habit from his friend, Thomas Hariot, a surveyor who, during an expedition to North Carolina, had seen Indians smoke the dry and powdered leaves from a clay pipe. "We ourselves tried their way of inhaling the smoke," Hariot wrote in his *Brief and True Report of the New Found Land of Virginia* (1588). The group had "many rare and wonderful proofs of the beneficial effects of this plant, which to relate in detail would require a whole volume to itself."

Raleigh's First Pipe
(courtesy of New York Public Library)

Soon, thanks to Raleigh's zealous endorsement, smoking was the rage in late-sixteenth- and early-seventeenth-century England. Imagine how bizarre it must have seemed in the tobacco-as-medicine culture of sixteenth-century England the first time Raleigh lit up, puffing away on his pipe, just for the fun of it. Centuries later, the young American comedian Bob Newhart described the absurdity of it all in his classic comedy routine, *Introducing Tobacco to Civilization.* The audience hears one side of a conversation between the London-based boss of the West Indies Co., played by Newhart, and Raleigh, who has called to tell him about the discovery of a new plant called tobacco.

"Who is it? Sir Walter Raleigh from the Colonies? Yeah, yeah. Put him on, will you? (Hey, Harry. Pick up on the extension. It's nutty Walt again.)

"Hi, Walt, baby. How are you, guy? What is it this time, Walt? You got another winner for us, do you?

"Toe-back-o? What's tobacco, Walt? It's a kinda leaf. And you bought 80 tons of it. Let me get this straight, now. You bought 80 tons of leaves?

"This may come as kind of a surprise to you, Walt, but come fall in England here, we're kind of up to our . . . It isn't that kind of leaf, huh?

"What is it? A special food, Walt?

"Not exactly? It has a lot of different uses. What are some of the uses, Walt?

"Are you saying snuff, Walt? What's snuff?

"You take a pinch of tobacco, heh, heh, and you shove it up your nose? Ha, ha, ha. And it makes you sneeze, huh? I imagine it would, Walt, yeah.

"It has some other uses, though? You can chew it? Or put it in a pipe? Or you can shred it up and put it on a piece of paper, and roll it up, heh, heh, heh, and . . .

"Don't tell me, Walt. Don't tell me. You, you stick in your ear, right, Walt? Ho, ho, ho, heh, heh, heh . . .

Oh! Between your lips! Then what do you do to it, Walt? You . . . ha, ha, ha . . . you set FIRE to it! And you inhale the smoke."

(Pause)

"Say Walt, we've been a little worried about you. Ever since you put your cape down over that mud. Walt, I think you're gonna have a tough time getting people to stick burning leaves in their mouths. . . . "[2]

Smoking *is* a strange habit. Nobody really knows how or why man first came up with the idea of setting fire to a batch of brown tobacco leaves and then sucking the acrid smoke down into his lungs. It most likely happened first in the Americas, where the plant originated, and many historians think the use of smoking in religious rituals dates back at least to the Mayan civilization in

Central America during the first century B.C. But where they got the idea remains a mystery.

Sparking an Industry

The widespread popularity of tobacco for pleasure as advocated by Raleigh soon gave rise to tobacco as an industry. In the late sixteenth century, Spain, which had funded Columbus's trip to the New World, reaped the spoils of the tobacco discovery and controlled the world tobacco market, cultivating high-quality tobacco plants in its settlements in the West Indies and South America. Although the American colonists had access to their own tobacco leaves, a variety known as *Nicotiana rustica*, smokers cringed at the bitter taste, preferring instead the sweeter-tasting *Nicotiana tobaccum* proffered by Spain.

It was John Rolfe, future husband of Pocahantas and booster of the fledgling Jamestown colony, who came up with the idea to give up on *Nicotiana rustica* and import some tobacco seeds from the West Indies. The plants flourished in the Virginian soil, and in 1613, the colony sent its first shipment of tobacco to England. It was the first sign that the struggling colony could have commercial importance. The Jamestown colonists were hooked. They planted tobacco in virtually every open space, neglecting food production, home building, and even their water wells as they tended the new cash crop.

Indeed, for better or worse, tobacco built America. The search by tobacco growers for new fertile land pushed the original boundaries of the colonies to the south and west. Tobacco changed the social fabric of the south, creating large plantations and a ruling class of wealthy land owners, which in turn helped foster a stronger sense of independence among the Southern colonists. The search for cheap labor to tend to the plants fueled the African slave trade long before cotton was king. Tobacco was used to pur-

A Tobacco Plantation
(courtesy of New York Public Library)

chase slaves from European traders, and tobacco was even used to bribe Africans to assist the slave traders in rounding up their countrymen. And because the American tobacco trade was so lucrative for the English crown, tobacco played a crucial factor in the American Revolutionary War. After all, from England's perspective, tobacco made the colonies worth fighting for, and the Americans, who, among other reasons, were annoyed that the crown was controlling their tobacco trade, funded the war largely with loans from France, using tobacco as collateral.

"Tobacco was the dominant element in shaping the social customs, the political and financial systems, the industrial life and the territorial growth of the Southern British colonies," writes tobacco historian Jerome Brooks. "The forces which were set in motion when tobacco was sovereign there affected the governments of Europe and the trade of the world . . . and remain powerful factors in the sociological and economic life of the U.S. to our own time."[3]

Although tobacco use spread rapidly in the sixteenth and seventeenth centuries, the cigarette made its debut much later. When the first explorers of the New World arrived, the Native Americans were using tobacco in much the same way it's used today—they chewed it, smoked it in pipes, wrapped it in leaves (like a cigar), or stuffed it in reeds (like a cigarette). Although the use of cigars and miniature tobacco tubes—known in Spanish as *papeletes* or *cigaritos*—caught on in Spain and Turkey, most of Europe's smoking culture centered on the pipe for more than two centuries following the discovery of tobacco in the New World. In eighteenth-century France, amidst a fledging antitobacco movement (whose members opposed smoking tobacco, in part, because it was a fire hazard), fashionable tobacco users turned to snuff-powdered tobacco that was pushed into the nose. The use of snuff spread so quickly in Europe that the British literary figure Dr. Samuel Johnson, noting that scores of smokers had abandoned their pipes for snuff boxes, proclaimed, "Smoaking has gone out."

But smoking hadn't gone out, it just went underground. Snuff was the stuff of the upper class, and half the enjoyment came from the affectations associated with it. With great ceremony, aristocratic snuff users brandished their gilded and lavish snuff boxes before inhaling a pinch of the tobacco powder. But the French Revolution in 1789 put a damper on most aristocratic pursuits, including snuff. The revolutionaries, searching for something to replace the snuff craze, had taken to smoking the *cigaritos*, which were made from the leftovers of pipe tobacco, cigars, and snuff and were widely viewed as the poor man's cigar. In the early 1800s, smoking returned to western Europe in the form of the cigar after British soldiers returned from the Peninsular War, where they'd picked up cigar smoking from the Spanish and Portuguese.

Not until the mid-1800s, in the wake of the Crimean War,

did smoking fashion turn to the cigarette. British soldiers in the Crimea had picked up the habit of their *papelete*-smoking allies from France and Turkey. When the soldiers returned to England in 1856, they brought the habit home, and cigarette smoking caught on. One of the earliest businessmen to cash in on the English cigarette craze was a London tobacconist named Philip Morris.

But it was across the ocean, in the new United States, that the cigarette would become an industry. As Philip Morris was rolling the first English cigarettes, the Americans were engaged in a civil war (1861–65). Tobacco played a significant role in the war, which was partially funded in the South by tobacco revenues and in the north by a tobacco tax. The American Civil War also marked the first time a government (the Confederacy) issued tobacco rations to its soldiers. And just as soldiers fighting in the Crimea introduced England to the cigarette, the mingling of soldiers from the South with soldiers from the North, where the cigarette was just showing up in big cities, aided the spread of the cigarette in the United States.

Still, for most of the nineteenth century, tobacco users stuck to chewing tobacco or smoking cigars or pipes. The skill needed to make cigarettes limited the growth of the industry. Even the best cigarette rollers could make only about four cigarettes a minute.

After the Civil War, a former Confederate soldier named Washington Duke had taken what remained of his family farm—a few tobacco leaves—and turned it into a family pipe-tobacco business. At the time the cigarette was still a novel way to enjoy tobacco; the chewing "plug" was the most popular method. But competition from other brands, particularly the Bull Durham brand of plug tobacco, sent Duke searching for a new niche. Washington Duke's oldest son, James Buchanan "Buck" Duke, saw the potential of the cigarette, which, though still a tiny market, was gaining popularity in England and New York. In 1881, he introduced Duke of Durham cigarettes.

When Buck Duke heard that a Virginian named James Bonsack had patented a cigarette-making machine, he gambled that machine-made cigarettes were the wave of the future. In 1884, after some initial start-up problems, Buck Duke's Bonsack machines were spitting out cigarettes. The machine, which sliced cigarettes from an endless tube of wrapped tobacco, produced 200 cigarettes a minute, and it could make as many cigarettes in a day as 40 hand rollers. The cost savings were huge—just 30 cents for a machine-made cigarette, less than half the 80 cents it cost to make a hand-rolled cigarette.[4] Mass production allowed Duke to undercut his competitors, who initially rejected the idea of machine-made cigarettes, believing smokers preferred the quality of a handmade smoke.

W. Duke & Sons also was among the first cigarette makers to engage in the promotion and marketing of cigarette brands, a hallmark of the industry today. Duke brands came with collectible cigarette cards with pictures of athletes and actresses as well as coupons to reward customers for bulk purchases. A roller-skating team, dubbed the "Cross Cuts" after one of the company's brands, even toured towns, generating free publicity for Duke brands.

As Buck Duke's sales increased, so did his ambition to dominate the U.S. and, ultimately, the world cigarette market. He bought out his rivals, including Richard Joshua Reynolds, the founder of R.J. Reynolds Tobacco Co. In 1890, Duke consolidated his empire under the name American Tobacco Co., which controlled 90 percent of the U.S. cigarette business and an estimated two-thirds of the pipe, snuff, and chewing tobacco sales. Nonetheless, the ambitious tobacco man greedily gazed across the Atlantic at the burgeoning cigarette business in Europe.

In 1901, Duke reportedly scheduled a meeting with more than a dozen of the top tobacco firms in England and brashly introduced himself: "Hello boys. I'm Duke from New York, come to take over your business."[5] To counter the crass American, 13 British companies formed the Imperial Tobacco Co. (Philip

Morris, incidentally, didn't join the group, but instead decided to push its own brands in the United States, forming Philip Morris Corp. in New York in 1902.) The formation of Imperial Tobacco resulted in a transatlantic tobacco war, as the two groups began cutting prices and offering bonuses to British tobacco retailers even as the British tobacco giant sought to gain a foothold in the United States. But soon, both sides had had enough. In 1902, Imperial Tobacco and Duke's American Tobacco called a truce, joining together to form the British American Tobacco Co.

For nearly a decade, the alliance flourished. At the same time, however, Duke's tobacco trust received unwelcome attention in America. A growing antitrust climate, fueled by trust-busting president Theodore Roosevelt, had triggered a backlash against Duke. In the summer of 1907, the *Raleigh News and Observer* launched a vitriolic attack. "The trust's desires are modest. All it wants is the earth with a barbed wire fence around it."[6]

In 1911, the U.S. Supreme Court ordered Duke to dismantle his empire. R.J. Reynolds, Lorillard, Liggett & Myers, among other tobacco companies, were released from Duke's grasp. Nonetheless, today's tobacco firms owe much of their success to Buck Duke's efforts to modernize the cigarette industry.

Cigarette Culture

While Buck Duke modernized cigarette production, Richard Joshua Reynolds modernized the cigarette. Ironically, cigarettes were the part of the tobacco business Reynolds liked the least. He preferred chewing tobacco and even harbored fears that cigarette smoking was unhealthy. But after laboratory studies assured him the product was safe, Reynolds, newly emancipated from Duke's tobacco trust, set out to capture a share of the cigarette market.

In 1913, Reynolds came up with the blend of tobaccos that would forever change the cigarette. The blend was modeled after pipe tobacco and contained a mixture of domestic and Turkish leaf as well as some flavoring additives. The result was a distinctive smoke richer than domestic blends and lighter than Turkish varieties.

But Reynolds's most significant move was his decision to put his efforts behind just one brand, something unheard of at the time. Although about 50 brands dominated the market, the leader was Liggett & Myers' "Fatima," billed as a Turkish blend. With his sights set on Fatima, Reynolds decided he needed a name equally reminiscent of the Orient. He considered the names "Kismet," "Nabob," and "Kamel," but in the end, he chose "Camel." A Barnum & Bailey circus camel named Old Joe served as a photographer's model for the brand, and Reynolds generated excitement for the new smoke with advertisements that exclaimed "The Camels Are Coming." Within a year the new brand had captured 13 percent of the market.[7] But more important, Camels spawned a new age in the cigarette business, in which manufacturers concentrated their sales and promotion efforts behind a few key brands.

By 1919, a year after the death of Richard Joshua Reynolds, cigarettes were consuming more pounds of tobacco leaf than was pipe tobacco. Three years later it overtook chewing tobacco as the fastest-growing tobacco product. One reason for the shift is that the cigarette was simply better suited to the urban lifestyle of the twentieth century. Chewing tobacco is a messy, dirty habit. Despite the presence of spittoons in public gathering places, spitting in public fell out of fashion as city dwellers began worrying about diseases (like tuberculosis) that came with crowded urban life. Cigars and pipes produced a heavy, smelly odor, and, because they took a while to smoke and often occupied both hands, they were considered leisurely pursuits that didn't fit the hustle and bustle of the industrial age. By contrast, the cigarette was a light and fast smoke, easy to use while working in an office or for a quick fix on break from work at the factory. Per capita consumption more than doubled from 173 smokes a person in 1911 to 395 cigarettes in 1916.[8] But the gains cigarette makers saw in those early years of the cigarette would pale in comparison to what lay ahead, as the drum beats of war promised to introduce legions of new smokers to the cigarette.

At the height of America's involvement (1917–18) in World War I, American General John J. Pershing sent an urgent cable to Washington, D.C. "You ask me what we need to win this war. I answer tobacco as much as bullets."[9] How could a cigarette be as important to a soldier as his weapon? On the battlefield, a cigarette helps a soldier endure the tedium of war. It can steady nervous hands, calm the wounded, and provide its user with a quick hit of courage. No other tobacco product is as suited to battle as the cigarette. Pipes often require two hands and cigars, because they often need to be re-lighted, are too much of a distraction. The confined space of a foxhole makes chewing tobacco, and the spitting that goes with it, impractical. But the cigarette is compact, relatively clean, and easy to share in the trenches. Moreover, as Richard Klein argued in *Cigarettes Are Sublime* (1993), it is also spiritually suited to the battlefield:

> *Cigarettes free the soldier by momentarily masking the cruelty of his condition; their effect is less that of producing a narcotic sensation than of permitting an intellectual stance detached from reality—one that, Janus-like, invites the return of nostalgia or speculates in dreamy anticipation. But cigarettes are more than therapy. It is not enough merely to assert that though bad for health, they provide remedies for ills of the spirit. In fact, cigarettes serve soldiers in other ways, more puzzling and in peacetime less apparent. Consider the enigmatic assertion of General Lasalle (1775–1809), a Napoleonic hero who, before he fell valiantly, at the battle of Wagram, is reputed to have said: "A hussard must smoke; a cavalryman who does not smoke is a bad soldier." What does this mean? The general's claim that there is a link between smoking and being a good soldier is not argued; it is merely asserted, apodictically, like one*

of those mute Marlboro or Camel advertisements that show
only the vivid image of a man clearly accustomed to pitting his
strength against the forces of nature.

At times in recent history refusing to smoke was considered
anti-American, a rejection of a certain idea—some might call
it a myth—of the heroic linked to the pathos of the frontier. By
heroism is meant in the strict Hegelian sense, courage in the
face of death, looking death in the face. When one smokes, one
does not merely suck a tit of consolation; cigarette smoke is not
always, not often, perhaps never mother's milk—it mostly tastes
bad, produces a faint nausea, induces the feeling of dying a lit-
tle every time one takes a puff. But it is the poison in cigarettes
that recommends them to the heroic—a strong poison; it takes
an infinitesimally smaller amount of nicotine to kill an adult
than it does of, say, heroin or cocaine. In every puff there is a
little taste of death, which makes cigarettes the authentic disci-
pline of good soldiers.[10]

While the cigarette has given comfort to soldiers at war, the
very act of war has played a unique role in the spread of tobacco,
particularly the cigarette. The Crimean War and the American
Civil War aided the spread of the cigarette, and World War I is said
to have turned thousands of nonsmoking young men into regular
cigarette smokers. Before the war, cigarette smoking was viewed as
slightly effeminate. But during World War I, cigarettes "quickly
became the universal emblem of the camaraderie of mortal com-
bat, that consummate male activity," writes Richard Kluger in
Ashes to Ashes (1997).[11]

Not only did war introduce scores of young nonsmokers to
the tobacco habit, but it also stifled antitobacco efforts, as citizens
focused on more weighty matters of national security and the safe-
ty of their fathers, sons, and husbands. During World War I, vehe-
ment tobacco opponents like the Red Cross and the Young Men's
Christian Association (YMCA) even helped supply cigarettes to

Red Cross Distributes Cigarettes to Soldiers
(© Hulton-Deutsch Collection/Corbis)

soldiers on the battlefield. By 1919, U.S. consumption soared annually to 727 cigarettes for every adult.[12]

During World War II (1941– 45), President Franklin D. Roosevelt legitimized smoking by declaring tobacco an essential wartime crop. Even Army training manuals of the day urged leaders to "smoke and make your troopers smoke." Gen. Douglas MacArthur himself demanded a better supply of tobacco in the soldier's daily ration. He ordered that $10 million raised for the war effort "be used to purchase American cigarettes, which, of all personal comforts, are the most difficult to obtain here."[13]

For their part, the tobacco companies were happy to oblige, although wartime shortages sometimes made it difficult. During World War I, ingredients such as the artificial sweetener saccharin, which was made from the same substance as an ingredient in TNT, were in short supply. During World War II, the American Tobacco Co., according to company lore, faced a shortage of chromium, which was used to make the green ink in the famous

Average Cigarette Consumption Per Adult in Industrialized Countries, 1920-1990

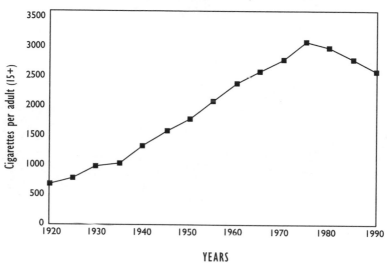

green Lucky Strike label. As a result, the color of the package was changed to white with the slogan "Lucky Strike Green Has Gone To War . . . so here's the smart new uniform for fine tobacco." The timing of the ink shortage was fortuitous. Company research had shown that women didn't like the green packaging because it often clashed with their clothes. Winning women smokers to the brand, research showed, would require a more neutral color, such as white.[14]

But for all the hurdles war imposed on cigarette production, smoking increased dramatically during war years. A study in 1918 found that wartime soldiers use 60 to 70 percent more tobacco than in peacetime. And even civilians at home sought solace in tobacco, smoking 15 to 20 percent more than usual.[15] In 1941, just before the U.S. entry into World War II, Americans smoked annually an average of 2,236 cigarettes each, including the tax-free cigarettes shipped to the armed forces. By 1945, that number had risen 48 percent, to 3,449 [See Fig. 1].[16]

Harvard anthropologist Dr. Earnest Albert Hooton tried to explain the nation's incessant craving for cigarettes. "The boys in the foxholes, with their lives endangered, are nervous and miserable and want girls. Since they can't have them, they smoke cigarettes. The girls at home, with their virtue not endangered, are nervous and miserable and want boys. Since they can't have them, they too smoke cigarettes."[17]

While war and the new wave of cigarette advertising and branding solidified the cigarette's survival as an industry, it was in the prosperity of the postwar years that the cigarette became an intrinsic part of contemporary culture. Indeed, cigarettes were well suited to the heady days after the war, when both Americans and Europeans, driven by a sense of entitlement following years of wartime suffering, indulged in cigarettes as a seemingly harmless vice. During the war, Hollywood had propelled this cigarette culture with celluloid images of seductive cigarette smoke spiraling from the lips of screen sirens like Lauren Bacall and Bette Davis. The silver screen helped transform smoking from an enjoyable pastime to a marker of mood and image. Trying to figure out who's the free-spirited hero, the rebel, or the wayward woman? Look for the cigarette.

By the 1950s, the first news reports that smoking might cause health problems began to appear. But the bad news seemed to enhance, rather than diminish, the cigarette's role in popular culture. The fact that there was growing unease about cigarettes affirmed the cigarette's role as seductive right of passage for rebellious teenagers. The leather-clad, cigarette-smoking outsider, immortalized by James Dean in *Rebel Without a Cause*, appealed to a generation that had grown disillusioned with cookie-cutter suburbs and the *Ozzie and Harriet* lifestyle. Advertisers responded with rugged, adventurous pitchmen like the Marlboro Cowboy in a bid to tap into the cigarette smoker's psyche. "Cigarettes are very bad for you, it is true," notes Cornell professor and author Richard Klein. "But it's only a half truth if it isn't accompanied by the proposition that by being bad, cigarettes are also very good."[18]

Concerns about the health risks associated with smoking, fueled by the first report on tobacco from the U.S. Surgeon General in 1964, finally began to take a toll on smoking rates in the 1960s and 1970s. But the growing prohibition against smoking wasn't enough to counter the cigarette's image as both a glamorous accoutrement and a rebellious torch. The most glamorous woman of the day, First Lady Jacqueline Kennedy, was often pictured with cigarette in hand, lending a sense of sophistication and class to the habit.

And the troubled, antiestablishment tenor of the sixties and seventies seemed custom-made for the smoker's personality. Studies have shown that smokers are more likely to take risks, act defiantly, and rebel against cultural norms than are nonsmokers. Smokers, for instance, are less likely to wear seat belts and more likely to be divorced. They are even said to have higher sex drives.[19] So while government health warnings and growing antitobacco sentiments certainly scared many smokers off the habit, those very prohibitions also served to solidify many smokers' loyalties, partly because the more smoking was vilified, the more rebellious and appealing it seemed. "Smoking has always been somewhat daring and has become much more so since the 1960s," writes David Krogh in *Smoking: The Artificial Passion* (repr. 1992). "There's a commercially approved way of being daring, and it's called smoking cigarettes."[20]

More recently, as the tobacco industry has come under increasing attack by politicians, lawyers, and antismoking crusaders, cigarettes have emerged as a torch of individuality, a symbol that its user isn't swayed by political correctness or the hard-bodied health culture of the late twentieth century. As smokers have been pushed

FIGURE 2:
Timeline of Tobacco History

1492 – Columbus brings tobacco seeds from the Americas to Europe.

1586 – First recorded tobacco warnings labeling it a "violent herb."

1604 – England's King James I publishes his "Counter Blaste to Tobacco" under a pseudonym.

1613 – Virginia colony sends its first tobacco shipment to England.

1638 – China punishes tobacco use by death.

1665 – Europeans battle the Great Plague by smoking.

1761 – First recorded study of tobacco warns that snuff causes cancer of the nose.

1776 – The American Revolution is partially funded by loans backed by tobacco.

1826 – Nicotine is isolated as a compound.

1827 – The match is invented.

1839 – A slave inadvertently creates "bright" tobacco.

1856 – Soldiers returning from Crimean War introduce cigarette in England.

1880 – The Bonsack cigarette-rolling machine is patented.

1890 – Buck Duke creates the American Tobacco Co.

1906 – Lobbying by tobacco industry removes nicotine from the list of FDA-regulated drugs.

1911 – Buck Duke ordered to dismantle his cigarette empire.

1913 – R.J. Reynolds creates the modern blended cigarette and launches Camels.

1917 – Rations to World War I soldiers include cigarettes.

1941–1945 Tobacco supplied to U.S. soldiers in World War II.

1951 – Philip Morris sponsors the *I Love Lucy* show.

1955 – Marlboro is relaunched with the Marlboro Man ad campaign.

1964 – First U.S. Surgeon General's report on smoking.

1966 – Health warnings on cigarette packs begin.

1971 – Cigarette advertising banned from U. S. television.

1973 – Arizona passes the first state law restricting smoking in public places.

1977 – First Great American Smokeout.

1984 – Tobacco companies disclose 499 ingredients in a cigarette.

1987 – Congress bans smoking on flights of less than two hours.

1994 – FDA declares its intent to regulate nicotine as a drug.

1994 – Representative Henry Waxman's hearings prompt tobacco execs to deny cigarettes are addictive.

1996 – Liggett Group reaches settlement with plaintiffs' attorneys.

1997 – Tobacco industry agrees to $370 billion national settlement.

1998 – Tobacco industry reaches multi-state settlement worth $246 billion

2000 – Supreme Court rules that FDA lacks authority to regulate tobacco.

out of restaurants and forced to smoke in huddled masses outside office buildings, some avowed smokers say the trend portends a new era of intolerance and despotism. As a result, the very act of smoking now represents a backlash against the sanctimonious tone of the public health crusaders and anyone else who would threaten the right to life, liberty, and the pursuit of pleasure. Indeed, antitobacco efforts appear to be fanning the flames of rebellion in some camps—smoking rates among youths began to rise again in the late 1990s,[21] fueling speculation that the cigarette is poised for a resurgence. "Cigarettes calm, they comfort, they give pleasure," writes Donald Gould in the *New Scientist*. "They act as a kind of stockade, a visible barrier between the naked individual and a hostile perplexing world."[22] [See Fig. 2]

2.

Money to Burn:
The Business of Cigarettes

*"I'll tell you why I like the cigarette business.
It costs a penny to make. Sell it for a dollar. It's addictive.
And there's fantastic brand loyalty."*
—WARREN BUFFETT

The Cigarette Economy

The world is hooked on cigarettes.

And it's not just smokers from the United States to China who can't get enough of the habit. For every smoker who lights up a cigarette, there are countless others who have already taken a long, slow draw from the cigarette economy. Politicians, government workers, store clerks, truckers, farmers, educators, artists and doctors—indeed, virtually everyone inhales its smoke.

Follow that smoke. It starts in the tobacco fields. In the United States alone, an estimated 142,000 workers, paid $929.8 million annually, are involved in the growing of tobacco. After the crop is harvested, it's auctioned off or stored in warehouses. Ring up another 11,000 jobs worth $162.5 million. Now it's time to roll the cigarettes—that takes 42,000 people and a $2 million payroll.

Farmers and tobacco factory workers clearly owe their jobs to cigarettes. But consider the truck drivers who transport cartons of cigarettes across the country, the dock workers who load ships with the precious cargo for export, and the retail clerks who ring up pack after pack of Marlboros and Kools and Camels. Then there are the industries that supply the tobacco industry with paper products, printing, fertilizer, construction, and a variety of other services. All told, more than 662,000 workers in the United States alone owe their livelihood—an estimated $15.2 billion in annual wages—to the business of growing, distributing, and selling tobacco products. The spiraling smoke of the cigarette business wafts through the economy as those workers pick up their paychecks and spend the money on more goods and services, creating another 1.15 million jobs worth another $39 billion in pay. Add up those direct and indirect jobs and salaries and you have $54.2 billion in U.S. wages—nearly 2 percent of the country's gross domestic product.[1]

So now the cigarettes are in the stores. What next? The tobacco companies need to convince people to buy them, so they spend more than $5 billion annually advertising cigarettes, creating jobs for ad agency workers, and magazine writers.[2] Philip Morris alone spends an estimated $165 million on corporate sponsorships in annually, funding countless museum workers, racetrack employees, and concert organizers.[3]

All this advertising makes people want to buy cigarettes, which in turn fuels the cigarette economy. Smokers around the world spend an estimated $300 billion on cigarettes, more than the gross domestic product of Mexico. If a country produced goods of that value, it would be ranked as the fifteenth largest economy in the world. In the United States, smokers spend $53 billion a year, which is more than Americans spend to buy clothes for their children ($26.9 billion), to eat at McDonalds ($16.4 billion), or to go to the dentist ($45.8 billion).[4] In the United States, federal, state, and local governments collect about $13.2 billion annually in tobacco taxes—$50 for every man, woman, and child.[5]

But there is more. Now that everyone is smoking, people are getting sick, so the smoke of the cigarette economy blows into the hospitals and doctors' offices around the world. The Centers for Disease Control (CDC) estimates that Americans spend $50 billion annually on smoking-related health care,[6] employing thousands of doctors, nurses, laboratory workers, and researchers. Thousands of firefighters battle nearly 23,800 smoking-related fires in the United States each year, fires that result in more than $300 million in direct property damage.[7] And the tobacco industry spends $900 million annually to employ a small army of lawyers, clerks, and court reporters to deal with tobacco litigation. The list goes on.

And then there's the antitobacco movement—advertisers, lobbyists, politicians, and health-care workers who dedicate resources to battling the industry. And what of the writers and publishing houses who have created books like this one—one web site lists more than 670 books about tobacco. Pharmaceutical companies have spent millions developing smoking cessation products such as nicotine patches and gum, with estimated annual U.S. sales of nearly $730 million,[8] which in turn create more jobs in the retail, advertising, health, and other sectors. The list goes on and on and on because the scope and size of the cigarette economy is immense and incalculable. But it's there, and without exception it touches every one of our lives. As Houston antitobacco activist Alan Blum once told the *Wall Street Journal*, "Everyone you know is once-removed from the tobacco industry."[9]

What price do we pay for the cigarette economy? The World Bank has calculated that because of health costs the world tobacco market produces an annual global loss of $200 billion. An estimated 3.5 million people each year die worldwide from smoking-related illnesses.[10] If they didn't die from smoking, certainly many would die from other causes. But what of those who wouldn't have?

How do you measure their contribution or cost to society? Smokers, on average, cut seven years off their lives. That's seven years of wages not earned, purchases not made, and vacations not traveled. "In human terms, I believe the cost is staggering," says former U.S. Surgeon General C. Everett Koop. "There are five million lost years of life by American smokers each year—that's a tremendous amount of living that is lost."[11]

Some economists, however, argue that society gains— at least financially—from the deaths of smokers who aren't around to drain the health-care system as they age. Cutting back smoking would "increase life expectancy (and) could lead to future increases in total medical spending," said economist Robert D. Tollison, in his 1994 testimony before the Senate finance committee.[12]

What of the $350 billion consumers around the world spend on cigarettes each year? If cigarettes weren't available, how would that money be spent? On food? clothing? education? University of Michigan economist Kenneth E. Warner examined a scenario in which tobacco disappeared from the U.S. economy. What would happen? Unlike similar studies sponsored by the tobacco industry, Warner's doesn't assume that money spent on tobacco would simply disappear. Instead, the average $2 a pack smokers pay would be spent on something else, and thereby redistributed throughout the economy. He found that within seven years of the cigarette's demise, the increased spending on nontobacco products would produce an estimated 133,000 *more* jobs nationwide than if that money were spent on tobacco. Although farming, manufacturing, and retail trade sectors would lose under his scenario, the stepped-up spending on nontobacco goods and services would lead to more jobs in transportation, communication, public utilities, finance, construction, and mining. He also assumes that governments would offset the tax loss with other tax increases.[13]

This is, of course, all theoretical. Nobody, including Warner, believes tobacco will disappear. But his study does support the ar-

FIGURE 3:
Minutes of Labor Needed to
Earn the Average Price of a Pack of Cigarettes
(based on average industrial wage)

COUNTRY	TIME (MINUTES)
Jamaica	44
Costa Rica	43
Belize	40
Portugal	33
United Kingdom	23
New Zealand	22
Canada	22
Norway	22
Ireland	21
Finland	21
Sweden	17
Italy	17
Greece	16
Australia	16
Denmark	15
France	15
Germany	13
Belgium	13
Netherlands	13
Luxembourg	12
United States	10
Republic of Korea	9
Switzerland	9
Argentina	8
Japan	6
Spain	5

SOURCE: World Health Organization estimates.

gument made by tobacco foes and health crusaders that the cigarette economy siphons off resources in the global economy, whether it's pocket money, the economic cost of cigarette-triggered fires, or something less tangible—like human lives. [See Fig. 3]

Merchants of Pleasure

Cigarettes are the envy of modern business. They benefit from three fundamental advantages over other consumer products. First, the production and sale of tobacco in cigarette form is an astonishingly low-cost, high–profit margin undertaking. Second, and perhaps most important, the cigarette is addictive and irreplaceable—there is no viable substitute that can steal away sales from a product that, by its very nature, has its users clamoring for more. And finally, the market is vastly expandable as cigarette makers target women, children, and developing nations.

"If you look at it as a business, it's phenomenal," says tobacco industry analyst David Adelman of Morgan Stanley Dean Witter. "It really has all of the characteristics that you would want if you were a business person saying, 'What's a business that's attractive where I would want to put my money?' Tobacco has high margins, high returns, pricing flexibility, strong established brands and behaves as an oligopoly. It's very much a growing global business around the world."

It costs surprisingly little to create that slender white stick of shredded tobacco leaves—just 18 cents a pack, including leaf, labor, packaging, and transportation. Throw in overhead costs, such as the manufacturing plant and equipment, as well as advertising and promotional discounts and even litigation expenses (including billions of dollars in recent industry settlements in the United States) and cigarette makers still enjoy underlying profit margins of 40 to 50 percent. The cigarette business is more than twice as profitable as other large-scale consumer products businesses, which post underlying profits ranging from 15 to 20 percent.[14] [See Fig. 4]

FIGURE 4:
Where Does All the Money Go?
Breakdown of the Cost of a $3.50 Pack of Cigarettes Purchased in New York City

Taxes:	$1.20
Retailer markup:	57 cents
Legal settlement payments:	41 cents
Givebacks to retailers and customers:	38 cents
After-tax profits to Philip Morris:	28 cents
Distribution costs:	21 cents
Advertising:	17 cents
Production costs:	16 cents
Legal fees for lawyers:	5 cents
Legal fees to state lawyers:	4 cents
Cash outlay to tobacco farmers:	3 cents

SOURCE: David Adelman. Morgan Stanley Dean Witter.

How can this be? Aren't tobacco companies under siege by lawyers and state attorneys general seeking to siphon billions of dollars out of the industry's pocket? Yes, they are. But this fact alone illustrates the marketing and financial savvy of the tobacco industry. It's true that for years the biggest variable in tobacco's financial equation has been litigation, but from a financial standpoint, the troubles aren't as bad as they first might appear. Tobacco companies aren't digging into their *own* pockets to pay for their legal wrangling—it's the smokers who are paying. And cigarette smokers, more than any other consumer, have shown that they are surprisingly willing to endure price hikes. In 1998, 15 cents of every $2.00 U.S. smokers spent on a pack of cigarettes—or about 7 percent of the cost—went toward legal and settlement costs. By 2000, the average price of cigarettes had surged 37 percent to about $2.75, and 50 cents, or about 18 percent of the cost, was paying the legal bill.[15]

In most industries, consumers wouldn't stand for those sorts of price hikes, but the cigarette merchants have a crucial advantage compared to makers of other consumer products: Most cigarette consumers are addicted, and a simple price hike isn't enough to stop them from coming back for more.

That said, it's too early to tell what impact the price hikes will have on smoking rates. The high prices could prompt some smokers to start smoking fewer cigarettes a day, causing a slight sales drop, but it's also likely that if prices surge too quickly, smokers will simply "trade down" to cheaper discount brands.[16] Nobody believes higher prices will ever snuff out smoking, and given the manufacturers' already fat profit margins and low costs, there is plenty of room for cigarette makers to offer short-term discounts and rebates to help ease consumers' sticker shock if necessary.

One of the most important components of the cigarette's success is the fact that by their very nature cigarettes spark continuous repeat purchases. The average smoker worldwide consumes one pack a day. Indeed, demand continues to grow even though many smokers are fully aware of the health risks associated with the habit. One reason is that, unlike most consumer products, there's nothing that can replace it. Soft drink makers face stiff competition from virtually every other drinkable liquid—wine, beer, juice, Kool-Aid, even water. Fast-food giants such as McDonald's and Burger King compete with local restaurants, grocery stores, and home cooking for their share of a consumer's stomach. But cigarette makers don't have to worry about their customers switching to alternative products. In the 500 years of recorded tobacco history, the cigarette has proved the most effective delivery device for nicotine, which is the reason smokers keep back coming back for more. Sure, there are several other forms of tobacco (snuff, chewing, and pipe), and there are other ways to get nicotine (pills, patches, and gum), but so far, nothing has emerged as a mass substitute for the smoking experience. This is partly psychological; smokers often are hooked on the process of smoking—holding the cigarette in their hand, raising it to their mouth, and sucking in. But there is a physiological reason as well: cigarettes deliver a more concentrated hit of nicotine to the body than does any other tobacco or nicotine product. "If you are going to raise the prices of donuts, maybe people would eat cupcakes or pies or candy bars," says Adelman. "But if you're going to smoke cigarettes, you're going to smoke cigarettes. There's nothing else like it. There's nothing that tastes like it. There's nothing that meets all the satisfaction you get from a cigarette."

The final chapter in the cigarette success story is about expansion. Cigarette makers have discovered they can increase sales among even existing smokers by using advertising and marketing to convince them to "trade up" to a more expensive brand, such as Marlboro. And children and teenagers will always be potential new customers. But the real opportunity to expand sales is in going global. Existing smokers in developing countries, for instance, tend to smoke more if they are offered Western cigarettes, which are less harsh, than if they smoke the cheap, bitter-tasting cigarettes made locally in many international markets. And developing nations offer a unique opportunity to cigarette makers because cigarette consumption is closely linked with social and economic change. When disposable income increases, cigarettes become more affordable, a fact that tends to increase smoking rates among young people. History has shown that millions of women now living in developing nations will start smoking as their economic and social status improves, particularly if they're exposed to Western-style advertising that promotes cigarettes as modern and liberating. For Philip Morris, which makes Marlboro, and Japan Tobacco's R.J. Reynolds unit, which makes Camel and Winston, international sales have quadrupled over the last 10 years, while U.S. sales are relatively flat. Overall, global cigarette

Biggest Tobacco Companies in the World

COMPANY	GLOBAL MARKET SHARE (%)
China National Tobacco Corp.	32.7
Philip Morris Cos. (USA)	17.3
British American Tobacco Co. (UK)	16.0
Japan Tobacco (Japan)	9.0
R.J. Reynolds Tobacco (USA)	2.0
Reemtsma (Germany)	2.0
Altadis (France and Spain)	2.0
PT Gudang Garam (Indonesia)	1.4
TEKEL (Turkey)	1.3
ITC (India)	1.0
Fortune Tobacco Co. (Philippines)	.9
Eastern Company (Egypt)	.8
Thailand Tobacco monopoly (Thailand)	.8
Lorillard Tobacco Co. (USA)	.7

SOURCE: Euromonitor.

sales jumped 20 percent between 1992 and 1996, driven by Western cigarette makers' push into new markets.[17]

So who are the companies that are peddling cigarettes around the world? There are five tobacco merchants who make 77 percent of the world's cigarettes. The biggest isn't even a company but a country—China, where one out of every three cigarettes in the world is smoked. China caters to its smokers through a state-owned tobacco monopoly, the China National Tobacco Corp. The biggest commercial producer is the New York—based food and tobacco giant, Philip Morris Cos., which, with its juggernaut Marlboro brand, has captured nearly 17 percent of the world cigarette market. British American Tobacco PLC (BAT), R.J. Reynolds Tobacco, the maker of Camel cigarettes, and Japan National Tobacco Co., round out the list.[18] The structure of the industry is typical in the consumer products business, which around the world tends to be dominated by a handful of international players, whether the item is food, beer, or paper products. In addition to the big world players, most countries boast their own major tobacco company. [See Fig. 5]

Philip Morris Cos.
1999 TOBACCO SALES: $47 BILLION[19]

Philip Morris, the man, was a London tobacco merchant who was among the earliest purveyors of hand-rolled cigarettes under the brand names Oxford and Cambridge Blues. Morris died in 1873, but the company continued without him. In 1902, the tiny firm opened a New York office, and by World War II the company was prospering and traded on the New York Stock Exchange.

Today Philip Morris is the world's biggest commercial tobacco company (not counting China's state-controlled tobacco monopoly), and its famous Marlboro brand is the world's best-selling cigarette, with an 8.4 percent share of the world market.[20] But tobacco accounts for just 54 percent of the company's revenues. "Big Mo" (a reference to its stock symbol, MO) has gobbled up a range of food and beverage businesses over the years. Its Kraft General Foods and Miller Brewing units sell everything from Kool-Aid to Miller Light. Most recently, it made a move to acquire Nabisco, the food company previously tied to tobacco rival R.J. Reynolds.

But it's more than just sheer size that distinguishes Philip Morris from the other tobacco companies. The cigarette giant is filled with brash, chain-smoking true believers. The company has been fearless in its efforts to fight back against growing antitobacco sentiments, whether fighting dying smokers in the courtroom or courting skeptics through the media. And with steady profit growth, Philip Morris has the most financial resources to fight the tobacco wars as well as boost promotional spending to grab market share. At the helm is chairman and chief executive Geoffrey Bible, an Australian who appears in the company's annual report smoking a cigarette. "We shall fight, fight and fight these issues," he was once quoted as saying about anti-tobacco efforts. "I can assure you we will fight with all the resources at our command because I am convinced we are right."[21]

British American Tobacco PLC (BAT)
1999 TOBACCO SALES: $30.4 BILLION[22]

Although regulators disbanded this transatlantic tobacco giant created by Buck Duke, this London-based tobacco company retained its focus as an international firm. Until the acquisition of Gallaher Tobacco in 1997, BAT didn't even sell cigarettes in Britain. Nonetheless, the company maintains a decidedly British demeanor, rarely taking the lead on antitobacco issues, instead choosing quietly to push its cigarettes in more than one hundred sixty countries.

BAT, like its rivals, eventually diversified, picking up businesses in the insurance and financial services industries. But in 1998, it spun off those businesses and now operates solely as a tobacco company. In 1999, BAT announced plans to acquire Rothman's International of Switzerland, which makes Rothman's and Dunhill brand cigarettes, giving BAT an estimated 16 percent share of the world market.[23]

BAT sells Kents, Lucky Strikes, and, in some countries, Benson & Hedges. But it is probably best known for its United States Brown & Williamson unit, which boasts the industry's highest-ranking defector, former research executive Jeffrey S.

Wigand, whose damaging testimony about the inner workings of the company set off the firestorm of state-backed lawsuits.

R.J. Reynolds Tobacco Co. (RJR)
1999 TOBACCO SALES: $7.6 BILLION[24]

A fierce takeover battle in the 1980s, chronicled in Bryan Burrough and John Helyar's book *Barbarians at the Gate: The Fall of RJR Nabisco*, left RJR saddled with debt and but a shadow of the once-wily tobacco giant whose Camel and Winston brands dominated the tobacco business before the 1960s, and before Philip Morris relaunched its now dominant Marlboro brand.

Founded by Richard Joshua Reynolds in 1875, the company pioneered much of the brand marketing that is the hallmark of the industry today. Indeed, the company's Joe Camel ad campaign became one of the most successful ad campaigns in the history of tobacco—and also the most detrimental. The cartoon camel became a lightning rod for antitobacco groups who were convinced cigarette makers were targeting children. RJR finally retired the campaign in 1996, but the damage to the industry had been done.

In recent years, the company has struggled to compete against Philip Morris's powerhouse Marlboro brand, although RJR's Winston remains one of the most popular international cigarette brands. The past few years have been tumultuous for RJR. In 1999, the company was spun off from food and tobacco conglomerate RJR Nabisco and is now a stand-alone tobacco company. The debt remaining from a leveraged buyout made it difficult for RJR to compete against its cash-rich competitors. As a result RJR in 1999 made the unorthodox decision to sell off its international tobacco operations for $7.8 billion to Japan Tobacco.[25] Although this move takes RJR out of the lucrative hunt for new smokers in international markets, the money allowed the

FIGURE 6:
Heaviest Smoking Nations
(by annual packs per person)

COUNTRY	PACKS PER PERSON
Greece	138.7
Japan	133.5
Poland	118.3
Slovenia	118.3
Czech Republic	111.9
Hungary	111.8
Switzerland	108.8
Slovakia	105.6
Germany	100.9
Spain	99.3
United States	95.2
Taiwan	85.8
Ireland	83.6
Austria	81.0
Australia	79.4
Belgium	78.3
Portugal	76.3
France	75.1
Great Britain	74.3
China	72.8

SOURCE: Euromonitor World Tobacco Report.

company to pay down its debt and better compete in the United States. Even so, sales volumes and market share have been slipping for more than a decade, and the $246 billion industry settlement, which led to higher cigarette prices, has taken a heavier toll on Reynolds than on the other tobacco companies. That's because Winston and Salem smokers tend to be older, and instead of paying higher prices they are more likely to switch to cheaper brands.

Japan Tobacco

1999 TOBACCO SALES: $29.9 BILLION[26]

The former state-owned tobacco monopoly of Japan, Japan Tobacco went public in 1994. Nonetheless, it's still a monopoly, with an 82 percent share of the Japanese market,[27] which boasts some of the world's heaviest and most dedicated smokers with a per capita smoking rate of more than 133 packs a year. (Only the Greeks smoke more.) [See Fig. 6]

Japanese consumers are far more tolerant of smoking than many consumers in other parts of the world, often choosing to battle the odor of smoke with perfume spritz and smoke-resistant fabrics rather than with a crackdown on public smoking. Nobody has sued the company for health-related claims, and even the antitobacco warnings are friendly. "Let's be careful not to smoke too much," reads the health warning on a pack of Japanese cigarettes.[28]

But Japan Tobacco has its share of troubles. With 84 brands, it lacks the focus and marketing savvy of Western competitors, who, now that some import trade barriers have been removed by the Japanese government, are making inroads into the market. Not only is the market mature and therefore difficult to expand, but Japan Tobacco, by law, also is restricted from buying tobacco on the world market, instead paying three times the world market price for the entire Japanese tobacco crop.[29]

To shore up its business, the company has diversified into pharmaceuticals and food and has begun to venture into untapped foreign markets, including the United States, where it sells low-priced cigarettes. Indeed, in the United States the company has a price advantage because it hasn't been sued and doesn't have to pay the heavy legal costs of various tobacco settlements. Most recently, Japan Tobacco entered the big time with its acquisition of the RJR international tobacco business. The move propelled the insular company into the top-three ranked tobacco companies in the world.

China National Tobacco Co. (CNTC)
1999 TOBACCO SALES: $23.4 MILLION (ESTIMATE)[30]

This state-controlled tobacco monopoly caters to more smokers than any other cigarette company in the world. One of every three cigarettes is smoked in China. But CNTC is more of a government agency than a business. It controls virtually every aspect of China's tobacco market, from the buying of tobacco leaf to the licensing of cigarette retailers. CNTC sells more than 900 cigarette brands, the biggest of which is Hong Ta Shan, which accounts for just 4 percent of sales. Although China accounts for one-third of the world's cigarette consumption by volume, it represents only 8 percent of world tobacco sales because of the low price of cigarettes sold there. CNTC doesn't release the actual value of its sales, but the $23.4 million estimate is based on the total value of the China market.[31]

Western companies are virtually drooling at the prospect of being allowed to do business in the tightly controlled Chinese market. For now, the CNTC controls all tobacco imports (except for the 2 percent of the market that is smuggled in) and has allowed only a few joint ventures and licensing agreements with Western tobacco companies. As a result, a limited number of brands, including RJR's Camels, Rothman's Dunhill's, Hong Kong's Nanyang Bros.' Double Happiness brand, and Philip Morris's Marlboro, are sold in China.

> In the United States, the business is even more concentrated, with four big firms producing 97 percent of the cigarettes. Philip Morris, RJR, Brown & Williamson (a unit of BAT), and Lorillard (which makes Newport, the country's most profitable cigarette) are known collectively as <u>Big Tobacco</u>.

Big Tobacco maintains its lock on the U.S. cigarette business through tight control of the distributors and retail stores that sell cigarettes. The big firms literally buy up virtually every inch of space in stores that sell cigarettes, dictating store displays, signs, and even the lowest-priced competitor that they allow to be sold in the store. This intimidating system of exclusivity agreements and promotional incentives to retailers makes it virtually impossible for new competitors to enter the market. The industry guarantees a steady stream of customers for its products with a barrage of image-oriented advertising—the industry spends about $5 billion annually in the United States alone promoting its brands.

The widespread opposition to tobacco, particularly in the United States, has created a siege mentality that—ironically—has made the cigarette industry one of the most stable, competitive rivalries in business today. In the 1950s, the top American tobacco executives banded together in the Tobacco Industry Research Committee to counter growing public concerns about the health hazards of cigarettes. The public-relations effort focused on recruiting doctors who didn't believe smoking was linked to cancer, discrediting writers who reported that it did, and even paying writers to place stories that were skeptical about the health risks associated with smoking. The Tobacco Institute, until it was recently disbanded as part of a litigation settlement, acted as a spokesman for the entire U.S. tobacco industry for more than forty years. Tobacco companies abroad have set up similar groups to speak on behalf of the international industry. More recently, cigarette makers in the United States joined together in an effort to negotiate a national settlement that would shield them from future damages.

None of this is to say that a rivalry doesn't exist; cigarette makers are constantly trying to boost sales by stealing share from competitors. But to many observers the cigarette industry lacks the cutthroat competition that is the hallmark of American-style capitalism. Computer makers and car manufacturers regularly slash prices, trash their competitors, and take advantage of a rival's misfortune. Makers of everyday consumer products regularly take potshots at each other, attacking Brand X in their advertising and exploiting public-relations opportunities. But tobacco companies don't like to rattle the competition or discredit their competitors' products. When one cigarette maker raises prices, the others usually follow. Each company tends to spend its energy and money touting the desirable attributes of its brands—and the industry saves the mudslinging for its real enemies, antitobacco forces and plaintiffs' lawyers.

The importance of this stable rivalry became obvious in 1993 when U.S. tobacco makers found themselves in the midst of a full-scale price war. Beginning in 1992, R.J. Reynolds, desperate to generate cash to pay off a mountain of debt, began pushing discount cigarette brands that sold for as little as one-third the cost of a premium brand like Marlboro. With the discount market thriving, Philip Morris stood to lose its dominance in the cigarette business. So on April 2, 1993, Philip Morris took the drastic step of slashing the price of Marlboro by 40 cents a pack. It also froze prices on all its other brands and took a $2 billion hit to profits.[32] The move hammered tobacco stocks on Wall Street and is now infamously remembered by tobacco shareholders as "Marlboro

Friday." "Everybody learned their lesson," recalls Gary Black, the Wall Street analyst. "You don't wreck the monopoly."

So, in short, here's the formula for the cigarette success story: Take a low-cost, high-demand product with no substitute. Drum up interest in your brands with billions of dollars worth of slick, glamorous advertising. Make it difficult for competitors to enter the market. Finally, keep an easy truce with rivals who are already selling the product. That's how the cigarette companies do it, and there's no other business like it in the world.

A National Treasure

Who makes the most money out of cigarettes? Tobacco farmers? Cigarette wholesalers? Multinationals like Philip Morris? Not even close. Every time a smoker puts down money for a pack of cigarettes, the lion's share of it jangles into the pockets of *government's*.

Whether it's through the state-controlled tobacco monopoly of China or the heavily taxed smokers in Scandinavia, governments around the world are profiting from cigarettes. In western Europe, more than 70 percent of the retail price of cigarettes is tax. In Brazil it's 55 percent. In Australia and Japan, more than 60 percent of the purchase price goes into the national treasury.[33] In the United States, home to some of the world's fiercest antitobacco rhetoric, taxes are surprisingly low—about 40 percent of the money spent on a pack of cigarettes goes to federal, state, and local tax authorities. (In the United States, state cigarette taxes vary widely, from a low 2½ cents a pack in tobacco-friendly Virginia to $1.11 per pack in New York.[34]) These taxes amount to billions of dollars in revenues to national treasuries. In the United States, the $15.5 billion collected in tobacco taxes is about 6 percent of what the country spends on its public elementary and high schools. In China, the $10 billion collected in tobacco taxes is the country's largest industrial tax source.

Since the 1600s, when Charles I of England, one of tobacco's first

FIGURE 7:
Tobacco Taxes Around the World

COUNTRY	PERCENTAGE OF RETAIL PRICE
Great Britain	79.6
France	76.1
Belgium	73.7
Germany	73.0
Italy	73.0
Canada	71.9
Netherlands	71.9
Poland	64.0
Japan	63.0
Australia	62.5
Spain	61.3
Brazil	55.0
Mexico	53.0
Indonesia	46.0
United States	39.5
China	38.0
Russia	33.3

SOURCE: Euromonitor.

and most vigilant opponents, levied a 4,000 percent tax on tobacco, the tobacco industry and politicians have been strange bed-
fellows. Governments around the world often levy high taxes on
cigarettes as a way to stifle smoking. Yet at the same time, government
officials are often willing to aid the spread of tobacco. [See Fig. 7]

For instance, in 1966, two years after the U.S. Surgeon
General declared that smoking causes cancer and other diseases,
the U.S. Congress voted to send 600 million cigarettes as relief aid

to flood victims in India.[35] In 1978, just as U.S. Secretary of Health and Welfare Joseph Califano was launching a $50 million antismoking campaign, President Jimmy Carter promised North Carolina farmers that he would support tobacco subsidies.[36] In 1996, at the Democratic National Convention, Vice President Al Gore blasted the evil tobacco industry for killing his sister, who died of lung cancer. But during an earlier campaign speech in 1988, just four years after his sister's death, he appealed to tobacco-friendly voters in North Carolina, with a different story—the one about how he raised tobacco most of his life. "I want you to know that with my own hands, all of my life, I put it in the plant beds and transferred it. I've hoed it. I've chopped it. I've shredded it, spiked it, put it in the barn and stripped it and sold it."[37]

Today, governments around the world are under growing pressure from tobacco foes, such as the World Health Organization, to raise taxes as a means of reducing smoking rates. Some economists believe that for every 10 percent increase in price, smoking rates drop between 4.5 and 5.5[38] percent. But this is tricky taxing territory for governments, who see tobacco as one of the easiest and most lucrative ways to enrich the national treasury. Tax the industry too heavily, and governments risk a quick reduction in cigarette consumption—and tax dollars.

There is another problem with raising taxes on cigarettes. Tax hikes can lead to an increase in smuggling. The problem with smuggling is that the government is the only one that loses; the tobacco company still sells its product, the smoker still gets to smoke—but the government gets nothing. That was the costly lesson learned by the Canadian government in 1993, where steady tax increases in Canada triggered an epidemic of cigarette smuggling and even prompted some consumers to drive across the U.S. border to buy cheaper cigarettes. In the face of declining revenues, the Canadian government thought better of its tax policy and cut federal and provincial taxes between 30 and 50 percent. By 1994, cigarette shipments had surged by almost 50 percent, smuggling had been virtually eliminated, and Canadian tax authorities exhaled a sigh of relief.[39]

The tobacco industry is well aware that its product is a major source of revenue for governments in the countries where it does business. "One of the prime activities of this industry is in effect to act as a tax collector for the government concerned," Rothman's chairman Sir David Nicolson told the European Parliament in 1980. "I therefore think that they [governments] will proceed cautiously before they kill the goose which lays such a big golden egg."[40]

Foreign Currency

Given that smoking rates in the United States and Europe have stabilized at around 28 percent of the total population, the search for new smokers around the world is perhaps the most crucial element of the tobacco industry's business strategy. And no country's government has been more duplicitous in its public stance on tobacco and more complicit in its spread around the world than the United States. In the 1980s, to the horror of world health workers, the American government helped tobacco companies push their way into Asia under the guise of free trade. "At a time when one arm of the government was warning Americans about the dangers of smoking, another was helping the industry recruit a new generation of smokers abroad," wrote *Washington Post* reporter Glenn Frankel in a four-part series in 1996 that documented the U.S. government's seemingly hypocritical foreign tobacco policy.[41]

For years, U.S. tobacco giants Philip Morris, Brown & Williamson, and R.J. Reynolds were trying to get a toehold in Asia, but they had been shut out by state-controlled tobacco monopolies and onerous laws that had a disproportionate impact on foreign (Western) cigarettes. (Laws in South Korea and Thailand, for instance, made it a crime to buy or sell foreign cigarettes.)

Borgman Editorial Cartoon
(Reprinted with special permission, King Features Syndicate.)

Although this discrimination against Western tobacco was done in the name of public health, the truth was that all of these so-called health-conscious countries had their own state-controlled tobacco monopolies. In short, it was okay for the state to sell tobacco to its citizens, but it was a health threat for Western companies to do it.

This *was* an obvious affront to free trade, but health activists thought, so what? Weren't there bigger issues facing the U.S. government in Asia than cigarettes? And besides, there's nothing like an old-fashioned tobacco monopoly to warm the heart of an anti-tobacco health activist. Almost by definition, tobacco monopolies are inefficient bureaucracies that charge high prices for poor-quality cigarettes—harsh, tar-heavy brands that would make the most seasoned Western smoker cough. The result is that per capita smoking rates tend to be relatively low in these countries. Monopolies rarely advertise, so their cigarette brands aren't linked with image or fashion. In countries with tobacco monopolies, smokers tend to be older men; women and young people aren't that interested in the product. (A good example of this is China, where about 63 percent of the men but only 4 percent of women smoke. And the smoking rate is about 73 packs a person per year—far less than the 95 packs per person smoked by Americans.[42])

But all that changes when the marketing-savvy Western companies enter the picture. They create demand for cigarettes by pushing mild, easy-to-smoke American blends backed by image-oriented, aspirational advertising. Per capita smoking rates surge as existing smokers smoke more of the mild blends, and women and children, attracted by enticing images of emancipated women and handsome, successful men, start to smoke.

Even so, the office of the U.S. Trade Representative decided that the "no foreign smoking" policy throughout Asia was an issue of national importance. As a result, U.S. trade warriors and some U.S. politicians strong-armed governments throughout Asia, including Japan, Korea, Thailand, and Taiwan, threatening trade sanctions if the markets weren't opened to U.S. tobacco. Republican Senator Jesse Helms, who hails from North Carolina, the largest tobacco-producing state, wrote a letter to Japan's prime minister, setting market share targets for U.S. cigarettes in the country. "May I suggest a goal of 20% within the next 18 months," he wrote.[43]

The U.S. embassy in Seoul was also working on behalf of American tobacco. "No matter how this process spins itself out," wrote the embassy's commercial counselor George Griffin in a letter to Philip Morris in January 1986, "I want to emphasize that the embassy and the various U.S. government agencies in Washington will keep the interests of Philip Morris and the other American cigarette makers at the forefront of our daily concerns."[44]

Not surprisingly, Asian countries eventually changed their policies. U.S. cigarettes quickly flooded their markets. In Japan, cigarettes became the second-most advertised product on television, up from fortieth a year earlier. The Boston-based National

FIGURE 8:
Smoking Prevalence of
Men and Women Around the World

| | PERCENT SMOKING | |
REGION	MEN	WOMEN
African	29	4
American	35	22
Eastern Mediterranean	35	4
European	46	26
South-East Asia	44	4
Western Pacific	60	8

SOURCE: World Health Organization estimates.

Bureau of Economic Research estimated that, as a result of U.S. government intervention, the sales of American cigarettes were 600 percent higher in the targeted countries in 1991.[45] And the arrival of the American tobacco companies pushed up average per capita cigarette consumption by nearly 10 percent. "In a decade where American goods—from sweet corn to stereo components to semi-conductors—are losing ground in Asia, cigarettes represent a rare and fiercely defended success story," wrote the *New York Times* in July 1988.[46]

The push into new markets has dramatically changed the balance sheet of U.S. companies. Sales internationally have quadrupled and now account for about half of all tobacco sales by Philip Morris.[47] But the aggressive policy of U.S. trade representatives has been blasted by health crusaders, among them Surgeon General Koop. "I don't think that we as citizens can continue exporting disease, disability and death," he said in 1989.[48]

Nonetheless, Big Tobacco's march around the world continues. And the reason is simple. There are 1.1 billion smokers around the globe, but just 300 million of them live in developed markets like the United States and Europe. And in many ways, those markets have peaked. In the developed world, about 25 percent of women already smoke, but overall, smoking is on the decline in the West as some consumers begin to take heed of years of warnings about the dangers of tobacco.

But it's a different story in the developing world—markets such as Asia, eastern Europe, and India—where most of the world's smokers (800 million of them) live. In those areas, just 7 percent of women smoke. [See Fig. 8] Awareness of the health risks of smoking is also lower. As BAT chief executive Martin Broughton says, "Huge tracts of the world live in totally different environments than the U.S. and Europe, where a cigarette is a real pleasure, a real luxury for a lot of people."[49]

How exactly does a tobacco company conquer a new market? The formula is surprisingly simple and consistent around the world.

Step 1: Launch heavy lobbying campaigns to convince government officials to open the market to Western companies, whether that means easing import restrictions (as they did in Asia), eliminating price controls (Turkey), or selling off state-owned tobacco factories (eastern Europe).

Step 2: Invest hundreds of millions of dollars in the country, buying up state factories or building new state-of-the-art manufacturing plants. This accomplishes two things. First, it guarantees that cigarettes sold from these plants will be of far better quality than the cheap cigarettes spit out by the antiquated machines owned by tobacco monopolies. Second, there's nothing like a little economic development to keep the government on your side. Cigarette makers were heroes in economically challenged eastern Europe, where Western tobacco companies went on a shopping spree in the early 1990s. By buying up the older government tobacco plants, hiring workers, and funneling ad revenues into various media outlets, Big Tobacco literally shored up the economies of the region. In Russia, a cigarette shortage in 1990 sparked riots and protests against the government of Mikhail Gorbachev. The government, which for years had resisted the encroachment of Western tobacco companies, pleaded with U.S. tobacco makers to help stave off this tobacco rebellion. Philip Morris and R.J. Reynolds happily complied, sending in 34 billion cigarettes.[50]

Step 3: Create a cigarette that appeals to local tastebuds but is easier to smoke than the harsh, cheap cigarettes already on the market. In Hungary, in a bid to appeal to local tastes, this strategy resulted in the creation of Jan Sobieski III, a Western cigarette developed by BAT but named after a popular king. In Turkey, Philip Morris used imported American blend tobaccos, which have a naturally higher nicotine content than Turkish tobaccos. Then, according to the *Wall Street Journal*, the company blended a special high-tar version of Marlboro, with about 11 percent more tar than American-made Marlboros, to more closely match the high-tar cigarettes that most Turks smoked. Eventually, Philip Morris weaned Turks off the high-tar cigarettes, and Marlboros in Turkey now resemble those sold in the United States. But the company's reasons for making these changes were less than altruistic. Philip Morris wants Marlboro to have a consistent taste across continents, much like Coca-Cola and McDonalds opt for a signature taste around the world, insisting that the taste of a Coke or a Big Mac never varies from market to market. So although it was necessary for Marlboro to initially have a familiar taste to Turks, the ultimate goal is for a consistent, signature blend of Marlboro around the world.[51]

Step 4: Enlist local retailers to help sell cigarettes. This is a surprisingly new concept in much of the developing world, where big retail chains and sophisticated distribution networks simply don't exist. In the past, store owners in Turkey had to close up shop and pick up a supply of cigarettes themselves. Philip Morris simply started delivering cigarettes to the country's tiny mom-and-pop

Vietnamese Boys Selling Cigarettes
(©Tim Page/Corbis)

retailers. Sales people even showed up at the stores dressed like cowboys.[52]

Step 5: Spend lavishly on advertising. This is especially effective in developing countries where many consumers haven't even seen advertising before, let alone the potent messages of the tobacco industry. (Advertising is a Western phenomenon; state-owned monopolies don't have a need to advertise because they are the only game in town.) In addition to the kinds of tobacco ads seen in the West, cigarette makers are particularly creative with their messages abroad. In Hong Kong, smokers spend hours in line to trade empty Marlboro boxes for knapsacks and lighters emblazoned with the Marlboro name. In Taiwan, RJR sponsored a dance at a popular disco, giving free admittance for five empty packs of Winstons.

"The Soviet Union never had such advertising," Ukrainian health official Vitality Movchanyuk told the *Washington Post* in 1996. "People are used to it in the West. They have learned to sift through it for truth and lies . . . but our consumers are more psychologically vulnerable to being manipulated by slick advertising."[53]

For their part, tobacco companies argue that by moving abroad, they aren't recruiting new smokers, they are simply recruiting existing smokers to their brands. And because American cigarettes have filters and lower tar levels than most foreign-made brands, the push by Western tobacco companies actually benefits the health of these countries, they argue. "Smoking existed in these countries long before we existed," an RJR spokesman told the *Boston Globe* in 1996. "If we cease doing business in those countries, they'd smoke something—it just wouldn't be an American brand."[54]

To a point the argument is true. Existing smokers are recruited to Western brands, and many of the new markets already have high smoking rates. But the difference is that per capita smoking rates tend to increase after Western companies arrive. One reason is that Western cigarettes are milder and easier to smoke. The other is that advertising tends to recruit new smokers, particularly women and children.

With 350 million smokers—that's more smokers than the United States has residents—China is the brass ring among tobacco marketers. Cigarette sales in China grew more than 40 percent between 1992 and 1996, fueled by increased involvement of Western tobacco companies. Despite the huge numbers of smokers, China has a relatively low per-capita smoking rate and a low rate of women smokers. The China market, therefore, has room to grow. Although the average price per pack in China is just 26 cents, the Chinese have shown they are willing to spend a significant amount of their income on tobacco products. Monthly per capita tobacco spending is $8.99, compared to $2.81 for alcoholic drinks, $1.08 for soft drinks, 79 cents for sweets, and just 32 cents for baby food.[55]

For now, the Beijing government jealously guards its monopoly, relying on cigarette sales for 12 percent of its annual revenue. But the market is highly fragmented with, as we have seen, more than 900 brands, the largest of which captures only 1 percent of cigarette volume and just 4 percent of sales. Nonetheless, the state tobacco company wants the technology and marketing know-how of its Western compatriots, and as a result, they've embarked on a handful of joint ventures and licensing agreements with some Western companies. Already, these companies have launched extensive branding campaigns, plastering brand names like Marlboro and Salem on cafe umbrellas and clothing throughout China and sponsoring countless radio shows and sporting events. Currently, foreign cigarettes account for about 4 percent of the market, but as the country continues to develop and play a bigger role in international trade, it's likely that the market eventually will open to Western brands. And that prospect makes Western tobacco executives see dollar signs. "If any cigarette company could capture the China market," says longtime antitobacco activist Judith MacKay in Hong Kong, "it wouldn't matter if every smoker in North America quit tomorrow."[56]

3.

Seed to Smoke: Cultivation, Packaging, and Distribution

*"A tobacco product is in essence
a vehicle for the delivery of nicotine."*
—CLAUDE TEAGUE, RJR RESEARCH SCIENTIST, 1972

Cash Crop

As the world puffs away on billions of cigarettes each year, it's clear that the cigarette has seeped into virtually every aspect of our lives, from the taxes we pay to the movies we watch. But what's really in that white stick of rolled paper, and why are so many people hooked on it?

The modern look and taste of the cigarette can be traced back to 1839 and a farm in North Carolina. A slave named Stephen was assigned to tend the fire overnight in a tobacco curing barn, but he fell asleep, and awoke to find the wood fire had nearly gone out. Panicked, he threw some charcoals on the smoldering embers. As the barn filled with heat rather than smoke, the tobacco turned a bright yellow instead of dark brown. As it happened, this new "bright" tobacco was far milder than tobacco cured over wood fires. Luckily for Stephen, the farm's owners were pleased

FIGURE 9:
Average Value Per Acre of Various Crops

CROP	VALUE
Tobacco	$4,089
Sweet potatoes	$1,627
Peanuts	$755
Cotton	$623
Corn	$278
Hay	$187
Soybeans	$170
Wheat	$140

SOURCE: Tobacco Institute, Washington, D.C.

with the result and even made a hefty profit on the unusual yellow leaf.[1]

It was an accidental discovery but a significant one in the annals of the tobacco industry. Not only did tobacco growers learn that the smoke-free heat from charcoal produced a more mild, flavorful tobacco, but more important, it was an early lesson that the industry didn't have to accept the tobacco that nature provided. By adjusting and altering the methods used to grow, cure, and manufacture tobacco, man could change the nature of the leaf, creating a smoother, more enjoyable, more potent smoke.

Growing tobacco isn't easy. It's one of the most labor-intensive crops around, gobbling up about 250 man-hours per acre harvested. By comparison, wheat takes only about three man-hours.[2] But tobacco is also among the most lucrative of crops. In the United States, an acre of tobacco will yield the farmer more than $4,000, while an acre of wheat nets only $140.[3] [See Fig. 9]

Three types of tobacco leaves—Bright, Burley, and Oriental— are the primary ingredients in most cigarettes. Bright leaf, also known as flue-cured leaf or Virginia leaf, is the tobacco created by the heat-curing process discovered by the North Carolina slave. Bright tobacco has an acidic smoke with a medium nicotine content. Burley is the name given to a tobacco leaf that started as a mutation in an Ohio tobacco field in 1864. Burley became popular because of its unusually absorptive nature, which soaks up sweeteners and additives used to flavor cigarettes and chewing tobacco. It has a fuller aroma and higher nicotine content and is air-cured in barns. Oriental tobacco is so named because it's grown primarily in Turkey. It has a harsh aroma and is cured in the sun.

Using these three tobaccos, cigarette makers have concocted primarily three different blends of cigarettes. The most popular, the American blend, is a mixture of all three kinds. Because Burley has a higher nicotine content than Bright or Oriental leaf, American blends such as Marlboro or Camel tend to have the highest nicotine kick. British-blend cigarettes use 100 percent Bright tobacco. Bright tobacco is the smoothest and sweetest of the three tobacco types, and British-blend cigarettes, such as Dunhill, Rothmans, and Players, are popular in Britain, throughout Asia, and in many of the former British colonies. The Oriental-blend cigarettes are popular in Turkey, eastern Europe, and the Middle East, but are quickly losing ground to American blends as Western tobacco companies make inroads in those markets. Although Oriental blends often are actually lower in nicotine than American cigarettes, they produce a harsh smoke that can make even a veteran smoker gasp.

The flavor of tobacco can vary greatly depending on the region where it's grown and the weather conditions. Sunny, dry areas tend to produce higher-nicotine tobacco leaf, while wet weather produces a milder leaf. As a result, tobacco companies often keep up to six years worth of tobacco on hand to ensure consistency in the blends and nicotine loads.

The tobacco cultivation process starts with the planting of tiny seeds that are nurtured into seedlings. This requires 50 to 100

First Published Illustration of a Tobacco Plant
(courtesy of New York Public Library)

square yards of plant bed for each acre of tobacco the farmer plans to harvest. About five months later, the seedlings are replanted in a tobacco field. The timing of the planting season around the world is dictated by warmer weather. In the U.S. southern states, the planting takes place in mid March but farther north the planting season doesn't occur until May or June. After blossoms appear a few months later, the plant is topped off to prevent all the nutrients from going into the flower and thus allowing the lower leaves to become larger and thicker. Once the flower is removed, small buds or "suckers" develop, which are removed by hand or with chemicals to allow the leaves to grow as large as possible.[4]

Soon after the blossoms are removed, the crop is ready for

harvest. Surprisingly, much tobacco harvesting is still done by hand, either by picking off the leaves or cutting down the entire stalk, depending on the type of tobacco. The Bright tobacco harvest takes place over a series of weeks, beginning from the bottom of the stalk and moving up as the higher leaves become ripe. Although hand picking still is common, mechanical harvesting is beginning to catch on in the Bright tobacco fields. The cultivation of Burley tobacco is almost entirely done by hand and is particularly grueling. Workers walk through the fields, hacking down the tobacco stalks and spearing them with a stick. The stick can weigh more than 30 pounds when full. On one Kentucky farm, workers earn 10 cents for each stick. Most average 80 to 90 sticks an hour, although faster workers can fill one hundred fifty.[5] But the picking of Oriental tobacco leaves, which are much smaller than other tobacco leaves, is painstaking. Workers pick the leaves and then literally string them together with a needle and thread, to be hung later from rooftops and trees to dry in the sun.

Even in this, its natural state, the tobacco plant can be toxic. Hundreds of tobacco workers each year become ill from an overdose of nicotine as a result of handling tobacco leaves. It's known as "green tobacco sickness" or GTS, and the symptoms, which last an average of two to three days, include nausea, vomiting, dizziness, abdominal cramps, and a rapid heartbeat. Although no widespread study of GTS has been conducted, one study in 1992 in Kentucky found that 10 out of every 1,000 tobacco workers in the state contracted GTS. In 1993, the illness had increased to a rate of 14 out of every 1,000 workers.[6] Some doctors think GTS might be even more prevalent, though underreported, particularly among migrant workers who increasingly are used to harvest tobacco. In addition, GTS is probably often mistaken for the flu or even pesticide poisoning. (Nicotine, incidentally, is sometimes used as a pesticide.)

Workers usually contract GTS when they harvest the tobacco leaves in the rain or before the dew evaporates from the leaves in the early morning. Nicotine is a water-soluble alkaloid, and when a worker's skin or clothing becomes wet, the nicotine leaches out of the tobacco leaves and is readily absorbed through the skin. "Nothing has ever made me as sick as working in green tobacco," says Jackie Scott, a Kentucky farmer who was hospitalized with the illness. "It can make you feel like you're going to die."[7]

Many farmers try to avoid the illness by letting their fields dry until about 10 A.M. and by staying out of the fields during and after a rainfall. Workers also change their clothes frequently, and some wear protective clothing such as long-sleeved shirts, chemical-resistant gloves, and rain gear.

But often, such preventative measures simply aren't practical in the day-to-day life of tobacco workers. Heavy clothing may protect them from GTS, but the workers are then at risk of heat exhaustion or heat stroke, given that tobacco is harvested in the hot summer sun. Many workers, especially those who take part in the labor-intensive harvest of the Burley crop, don't like wearing the bulky, cumbersome gloves out of fear of losing their grip on the tobacco spears and spiking themselves or a coworker. And tobacco is harvested on a tight schedule, making frequent clothing changes or postponements due to rain impractical.

Ironically, nonsmokers are more likely to become sick from GTS than smokers, who, because of regular use of tobacco, have an increased tolerance to the effects of nicotine. Young workers, who have less experience in the fields and long-term exposure to the tobacco leaves, are also more likely to become ill. However, no study has been conducted on the long-term health effects of exposure to natural tobacco leaves.

Once harvested, the tobacco is cured, either by using natural air (Burley), heated air (Bright), or the sun (Oriental). The air curing of Burley tobacco is the most time-consuming and labor intensive. Wagon loads of the speared tobacco stalks are driven to barns, where workers climb high on rafters to hang the heavy sticks in rows. This is also often the most dangerous part of the cultivation process, because workers must manipulate the heavy sticks while balancing on rafters twenty feet in the air. The Burley tobacco is cured by dry autumn air for four to six weeks while the yellowish leaves dry and turn reddish brown.

Nearly all of the tobacco produced in the United States is marketed at auctions, where baskets of leaf are weighed and graded. As is the case with virtually every stage in the making of a cigarette, the U.S. government has a hand in the tobacco-growing process as well. The U.S. Department of Agriculture imposes quotas limiting the amount of tobacco farmers can produce as well as a price-support program that guarantees tobacco farmers a certain price for their crop. If a farmer can't sell his leaf at the government's minimum price, he instead receives a government loan for the value of his tobacco. The tobacco is then taken as collateral by a government-funded cooperative and sold later, ostensibly when market conditions are more favorable, and the money from the sale is used to pay off the loan. The program has its origins in the Great Depression of the 1930s, when overproduction of tobacco caused prices to plummet and hundreds of American farmers to go out of business. For sixty years, growers of many other U.S. crops enjoyed similar price protection. In 1996 the so-called "Freedom to Farm" Act phased out various federal subsidies for most crops, including corn, barley, wheat, and rice. But three crops—peanuts, sugar, and tobacco—were exempt from the changes thanks to a powerful southern agricultural lobby. No doubt the price supports, particularly for tobacco, will continue to be targeted by opponents. Indeed, several lawmakers say it's hypocritical for the government to push antismoking measures at the same time as it shores up the nation's production of tobacco. But the debate has produced some unlikely allies. Because the nation's big tobacco companies would like to see the price of domestic tobacco decline, antismoking activists are taking sides with the farmers in a bid to keep the price support program intact as a way to ensure continued high cigarette prices.

FIGURE 10:
Tobacco Exports as a Percentage of Total Export Earnings

COUNTRY	PERCENTAGE/TOTAL EXPORT EARNINGS	
Malawi	64.11	($214 million)
Zimbabwe	23.46	($473 million)
Albania	7.17	($15 million)
Bulgaria	4.37	($229 million)
Burundi	4.21	($4 million)
Uganda	3.33	($7 million)
Greece	2.73	($389 million)
Tanzania	2.22	($17 million)
Oman	2.09	($121 million)
Brazil	2.03	($891 million)
Guatemala	2.02	($42 million)
Turkey	1.60	($439 million)
Honduras	1.14	($13 million)
Niger	1.04	($3 million)
Singapore	.96	($978 million)
Netherlands	.76	($1.4 billion)
Central African Republic	.76	($1.5 million)
Croatia	.76	($44 million)
Sierra Leone	.75	($1 million)
Sri Lanka	.75	($26 million)
United States	.70	($5.3 billion)
China	.68	($620 million)
Argentina	.68	($117 million)
Dominican Republic	.60	($14 million)
Syrian Arab Republic	.56	($27 million)

SOURCE: World Bank, Urban Development Department.

Even in countries without price-support programs, tobacco has proven a lucrative crop. Enticed by the big money to be earned from growing tobacco, thousands of farmers in India, Brazil, Zimbabwe, Indonesia, and Malawi have switched their fields—at times to their own detriment—from much-needed food crops to tobacco plants. The impoverished countries of the developing world have found it hard to resist the lure of the "golden leaf." In the tiny, poor African country of Malawi, tobacco generates more than 70 percent of all export revenue. Increasingly, small farmers, who were raising food crops to sustain their families, are shifting their tiny tracts of land to tobacco production. Today, about half of all tobacco production takes place on small farms, up from just 10 percent before 1990, according to the U.S. Department of Agriculture. But the money to be made in tobacco comes with a price. Formerly a food exporter, Malawi has begun importing food as a result of a growing population, adverse weather, and the widespread shift of small farmers to tobacco crops.[8] [See Fig. 10]

In Zimbabwe, in southern Africa, the government has actively promoted tobacco production on large farming estates, leaving the production of food crops to small farmers. In the early 1980s, Zimbabwe's commercial farmers produced about two million tons of corn a year. By the 1990s, corn production was down to 12,000 tons, as 80,000 hectares of farmland were diverted to tobacco production.[9] But the small farmers haven't been able to produce enough food to feed a growing population.

The switch has alarmed international aid groups such as the World Health Organization (WHO) because tobacco has proven to be a drain on vital resources in the developing world. In East and Central Africa, for instance, tobacco is blamed for forest and soil depletion, as huge areas of woodlands have been felled for fuel needed in the tobacco-curing process. The United Nations estimates that for every acre of flue-cured Virginia tobacco grown in developing countries, an acre of woodland is lost.[10] And an overconcentration on cash crops, such as tea and tobacco, has created a food deficit in the region. A study in 1992 by agriculture economists with the Southern African Development Countries found that ten countries in the region were posting population growth rates of about 3 percent, but food production was static or declining. Overall, about 0.3 percent of the world's arable land is in tobacco. If converted to food crops, that land would feed as many as 17.5 million people a year.[11]

But tobacco producers argue that tobacco money is an important fuel to the economies of developing nations, and lucrative tobacco sales allow farmers to subsidize the cost of growing food and irrigating fields. "Tobacco isn't just another cash crop here—it is the cash crop," says Raul Jose Ruschel, a leaf production manager in Brazil.[12]

And the major cigarette manufacturers—Philip Morris, RJR, and BAT—all have an interest in spurring tobacco cultivation in the developing world. In the U.S., price supports and powerful farm cooperatives keep the price of tobacco relatively high. But in the developing world, tobacco growers raise tobacco under contract at a price set by the tobacco buyer. For the tobacco companies, the savings is huge. The average recent price for Brazilian flue-cured tobacco, about 54 cents a pound, is what U.S. flue-cured was selling for in 1950, according to the *News & Observer* in Raleigh, North Carolina.

To guarantee a high-quality tobacco crop in the developing world, the cigarette makers have helped build the agricultural infrastructure in the region. Tobacco companies spend millions educating farmers about growing methods and have offered financial assistance to help farmers buy land and construct curing barns. They also provide the seeds, fertilizers, and chemicals used by the growers, giving the tobacco companies far more control over the cultivation process in the developing world than they have over U.S. farmers.

China is by far the world's largest producer of tobacco, but most of that leaf is consumed by the country's own smokers. The United States is a distant second in terms of production, but it's

FIGURE 11:
Where Tobacco Is Grown

COUNTRY	METRIC TONS
China	2,900,000
United States	688,222
India	562,750
Brazil	452,000
Turkey	229,400
Zimbabwe	207,787
Indonesia	177,000
Malawi	142,162
Italy	136,000
Greece	131,500

SOURCE: Tobacco Institute, Washington, D.C.

the largest exporter and importer of tobacco. The biggest fans of
U.S. tobacco leaf are Japan, Germany, the Netherlands, Turkey,
and Thailand. Most of the leaf imported by U.S. tobacco companies is Oriental leaf for use in American blend cigarettes, with
most of the supply coming from Turkey as well as from Greece and
Bulgaria. [See Fig. 11]

Crop to Carton

Once the tobacco is planted, grown, and harvested, the process of
turning it into a cigarette begins. Nowhere is the size and scope of
the world's cigarette industry more evident than in a cigarette factory. At the British American Tobacco factory in Southampton,
England, a continuous white rod of tobacco whizzes through one
of the factory's state-of-the-art machines. It is, quite literally, an
endless cigarette, destined for a seemingly endless supply of smok-

*Machine in
a Cigarette Factory*
(©Tony Arruza/Corbis)

*Factory Worker
Sorting Cigarettes*
(© Farrell Grehan/Corbis)

ers. This factory alone churns out 48 billion cigarettes a year—producing enough cigarettes in each working minute to supply a pack-a-day smoker for 24 years!

The modern cigarette machine has its origins in the Bonsack machine that revolutionized the industry. But while the first Bonsack machine spit out only about three cigarettes a second, the high-speed machines of today produce as many as 70 cigarettes a second. To create a cigarette, a mixture of blended tobaccos is funneled into the machine, which has been threaded with cigarette paper using a series of spools and rollers, much like the threading of a sewing machine or a film projector. After the tobacco and paper meet, in a blink of an eye the paper is rolled and sealed into a continuous tube of tobacco. Down the line, blades slice through the rod, cutting individual cigarettes. As the machine bumps and grinds and whirs, filters are attached. The cigarettes are then fed into an inspection device, which monitors the weight, length, and circumference. The machine spits out those that don't pass muster and feeds the rest into a packing machine. Once packed, the cigarettes head off to a vast network of wholesale distributors and retailers who sell the cigarettes to the general public.

But even though the manufacture of the cigarette is complete, the manufacturer's work is far from over. Tobacco companies work through distributors and retailers to ensure that their cigarette brand, rather than a competitor's, is the one that gets noticed first by consumers. Walk into a convenience store or cigarette outlet store. Virtually every inch of space where cigarettes are sold has been bought up by the cigarette companies. Whether it's that rack of Marlboro cigarettes on the counter or the big Winston sign at the front of the store, Philip Morris and RJR and other companies have shelled out hundreds of thousands of dollars to make sure the space is used exclusively for their brands—and that no other ads or products interfere with it. By buying up the store space, big tobacco companies make it tough for new

Clerks Preparing to Sell Cigarettes
(© Bettmann/Corbis)

competitors to enter the market. Just ask Jeannine VanDerVeer, owner of Red Hawk Tobacco Co. in Covington, Kentucky. She's tried to place her upstart Kentucky Blondes brand cigarettes in local tobacco stores, only to be told that the only available spot was a bottom shelf in the back of the store. "For the smaller companies to get in is really difficult," says Ms. VanDerVeer. "Every single bit of space is owned."[13]

The biggest tobacco companies all have their own incentive programs to encourage retailers to give their brands the best shelf space and store display. RJR calls it Retail Partners, while Brown & Williamson has dubbed their program Alliance Millennium. The most notable program is Philip Morris's Retail Masters— notable because it is said to be the most aggressive and lucrative of the retail incentives, so aggressive, in fact, that the Federal Trade Commission (FTC) has investigated Philip Morris's retail practices to determine if the company's methods unfairly restrict access for competing brands.[14]

Although other major consumer products companies, firms that sell soap, shampoo, diapers, potato chips, and cosmetics, all offer incentives and trade promotions to the retailers who peddle their wares, the practice is most pronounced among the tobacco companies. That's because, unlike Coca-Cola Co. or Procter & Gamble Co., tobacco firms can't promote their products on television. The best opportunity they have to connect with a consumer is in the retail store, where product displays, discounts, and the recommendation of the store clerk represent the companies' single best opportunity to convince a smoker to switch brands.

Under the rules of Retail Masters, a tobacco shop owner can display any tobacco brand. But to receive the sales incentives and bonuses of Retail Masters, a retailer gives the most prominent display to Philip Morris brands, and allows only temporary display of other brand promotions. Once a retailer signs up for Retail Masters, he earns "contract money" to pay for the floor and shelf space. The retailer also earns "flex funds," which are payments based on his sales of Philip Morris brands. The retailer uses that money to discount the price of Marlboro. As a result, Retail Masters retailers are able to sell cartons of Marlboro at prices that often are a dollar or more cheaper than rivals who don't take part in Retail Masters. This complex partnership between Philip Morris and its retailers is one way the company has maintained its worldwide dominance. The retailer stays happy because the program allows him to sell Marlboro for a lower price, which helps bring business into his store. Philip Morris wins because the store is filled with Marlboro signs and displays, and the retailer has an extra incentive to push Marlboro rather than a rival brand. The result: a consumer who walks into a Retail Masters store is inundated with the Marlboro message. If he already smokes Marlboros, the promotion and price discount will keep him coming back. If she's a new smoker, the cheerleading by the store clerk could prompt her to switch, or at least try Marlboro, helping Philip Morris lure one more precious smoker to its ranks.

What Have You Been Smoking?

The cigarette is deceiving. It looks pure and simple, just shredded tobacco leaves rolled in paper. But this slim stick of tobacco is a complex, highly manufactured product. Indeed, only about 60 percent of each cigarette is tobacco leaf. Another 30 percent is a filler made with reconstituted tobacco and chopped stems. (This 30 percent mixture saves tobacco companies money because it basically uses leftover scraps that would normally be thrown away.) The remaining 10 percent is flavoring and humectants, which help maintain moisture.[15]

In 1994, U.S. tobacco companies were required to release all the ingredients that can be used in the manufacture of a cigarette. The result was a staggering 599-item list of various flavorings and additives, most of which would require a chemistry degree to decipher. The tobacco companies point out that many of the ingredients are approved by regulators for use in a range of packaged foods. (Health critics counter that the ingredients are approved to be eaten, not smoked.) Nonetheless, many of the ingredients sound delicious—like sugar, cocoa, and licorice. Licorice, in fact, is one of the oldest cigarette additives. Spanish sailors used licorice water as a preservative and grew fond of the way it changed the taste of tobacco. That said, it's since been discovered that even seemingly harmless substances like licorice and cocoa can turn carcinogenic when burned.[16]

By far, the most important ingredient in a cigarette, from both the industry's and smoker's perspective, is one that occurs naturally: nicotine. Nicotine was isolated as a compound in tobacco in 1828, and tobacco makers like to point out that it is also found in tomatoes. Like the morphine extracted from opium poppies or cocaine found in coca leaf, nicotine is a powerful drug. A small amount is lethal, and it has occasionally been used as a weapon—nicotine darts have been used to shoot down elephants.

Most cigarettes deliver only about one milligram of nicotine. Nonetheless, studies have shown that the amount of nicotine in a cigarette would need to be reduced by 95 percent to stop its addictive power.

In *Smoking: The Artificial Passion*, David Krogh makes the point that nicotine, unlike morphine or cocaine, never "hit the big time" as an isolated drug, either for therapeutic reasons or for recreational use. The reason, he speculates, may be that smoking is simply the best delivery system for nicotine, while other drugs are more potent when injected. Indeed, he points out, it is the very act of *smoking* a substance that seems to aid the spread of it. Before the Chinese decided to start smoking opium in the eighteenth century, it was used primarily for medical purposes and sometimes for recreation. But once opium was smoked, addiction to it became rampant. And cocaine is far more addictive when smoked as crack than when inhaled as a powder. Scientists say smoking a substance helps it reach the brain more quickly than swallowing, inhaling, or even injecting it, and thereby helps fuel the addiction.[17]

In addition, the basic chemistry of nicotine may also be the reason that the cigarette has surpassed cigars, pipes, and chewing tobaccos as the preferred form for most tobacco users. As Richard Kluger explains in *Ashes to Ashes*, the dark leaf tobacco used in pipes, cigars, and chewing plugs is alkaline in nature, and as a result, is slowly absorbed by the alkaline environment of the mouth, where it has little impact on the rest of the body. But the mild smoke of Bright tobacco is more acidic and therefore isn't absorbed by the alkaline membranes in the mouth; instead, it travels down to the lungs, where the nicotine droplets are quickly absorbed into the bloodstream.[18]

When a person smokes, the nicotine in the cigarette reaches the brain, via the bloodstream, just seconds after being inhaled. There, like almost all addictive drugs, it causes the release of brain chemicals associated with euphoria and pleasure. Once the body's adrenal glands get their dose of nicotine, they release adrenaline. In this way, nicotine acts as a stimulant. The first cigarette of the day increases the body's heart rate by 10 to 20 beats a minute. "When the first nicotine arrives, the receptors for nicotine make the neurons very excited," says Dr. John Dani of the Baylor College of Medicine. "They are bursting with activity."[19]

Smokers also light up when they want to relax. Whether a calming cigarette is a psychological crutch or actually causes a physical change is in dispute. Research suggests that while nicotine can stimulate the production of adrenaline and euphoria-causing chemicals, in larger quantities it begins to block the chemical messages the body is sending, and, as a result, has a calming effect on its user.

In recent years, much of the debate about smoking has centered on whether the cigarette industry artificially controls nicotine levels to keep smokers hooked on its products. In 1994, an ABC News program, *Day One*, announced that it had uncovered the tobacco industry's "last, best secret: that cigarette companies manipulate nicotine levels to keep smokers hooked." The program claimed that Philip Morris "spikes" its tobacco filler by adding additional nicotine. Philip Morris sued ABC for $10 billion, and ABC later announced it would settle the case and issue a limited apology for certain claims in the report.

Nonetheless, the report for the first time shed light on the methods companies use to control nicotine levels, forever changing the national debate on cigarette smoking. Indeed, Philip Morris was so intent on refuting the "spiking" allegations that the company gave a plant tour to FDA officials and explained the blending processes and the methods companies use to control nicotine levels. In addition to using different types of tobacco with varying nicotine levels, manufacturers also focus on the "stalk position" of tobacco leaf. The leaves closest to the top have the most nicotine.[20]

In recent years, much of the focus on cigarette ingredients has been on the industry's use of ammonia. Ammonia hardly sounds like an ingredient that should be used in a product consumed by humans, but the chemical is valuable because it helps increase the potency of the nicotine a smoker inhales. This has become particularly crucial for tobacco companies at a time when health worries have prompted them to reduce tar levels in cigarettes. Because reducing tar also tends to lower nicotine, the cigarette makers needed to find a way to maintain the same level of nicotine delivery.

It would seem simple enough to add extra nicotine to boost levels of low-tar cigarettes, but internal industry documents show that the tobacco companies tried that and it didn't work very well. In *Smokescreen*, Philip Hilts cites a memo from the American Tobacco Co., which had looked into injecting additional nicotine into reconstituted tobacco. The company even came up with a code name for nicotine: Compound W. "An increase in the nicotine content of RC [reconstituted] tobacco by the direct addition of commercial nicotine does not improve the smoking and taste properties of the product," the memo reads. "The principal effect of the added nicotine was an increase in harshness of the RC tobacco without any improvement in the taste or aromatic properties."[21]

The tobacco industry claims that nicotine is important to a cigarette not for its addictive properties but because of its effect on taste. But various internal industry documents contradict that stance. A confidential Philip Morris document in 1992 compared the effects of nicotine to morphine and cocaine and stated that the primary reason people smoke is to deliver nicotine into their bodies. In a memo in 1972, an RJR research scientist wrote, "A tobacco product is in essence a vehicle for the delivery of nicotine," and he described it as "a potent drug with a variety of physiological effects."[22]

More detail has emerged from the testimony of Jeffrey R. Wigand, a former research scientist at Brown & Williamson, as well as from additional internal industry documents. Tobacco researchers have learned that much of the nicotine in cigarettes isn't released when the cigarette is burned but is chemically bound inside the leaf. According to a 1991 handbook for tobacco "leaf blenders," ammonia helps convert nicotine into a "free form" that has a greater impact on smokers. This "free" nicotine gets absorbed more quickly into a smoker's bloodstream.[23]

Philip Morris's use of ammonia to enhance nicotine delivery while reducing tar is widely credited as one reason for the rise in popularity of Marlboro cigarettes. In a bid to compete with Marlboro's success, BAT began its own work to genetically engineer a nicotine-rich tobacco plant that would allow the company to maintain nicotine levels while reducing tar. In the summer of 1977, a representative from BAT's Brown & Williamson unit approached North Carolina tobacco grower Lloyd Vernon Jones and asked him to grow some special tobacco plants on his eighteen-acre farm. Jones, happy for the extra income, complied and by 1983 two of the plant lines had survived. They were dubbed Y-1 and Y-2. Later, the Y-1 plant held up better under processing and became the focus of BAT's research effort.[24]

What makes Y-1 so special is the fact that it has a nicotine content of 6.2 percent, about twice the level of typical commercially grown tobacco. Industry documents show that BAT started growing Y-1 in Brazil to hide it from competitors and avoid the scrutiny of U.S. regulators. Indeed, before 1992, it was illegal to transport tobacco seeds outside the United States. The Y-1 experiment didn't always go smoothly. The high-nicotine leaf packed a hefty jolt of nicotine when smoked, making it too strong for many smokers. As a result, BAT researchers in England developed a technique to "puff" up the tobacco using liquid carbon dioxide. The puffed-up tobacco was more air than leaf, but when burned, it delivered a gradual nicotine hit.

Y-1 was more than just a laboratory experiment, it turns out. In a 1998 deposition, Roger Black, director of leaf blending for Brown & Williamson, testified that the company was using Y-1 in some of its cigarette brands. As a result, B&W issued a press release admitting that the nicotine-rich tobacco was being used "in small amounts in certain brands, like Raleigh, Richland, Prime and Summit."[25] These revelations have fueled criticism that the cigarette makers have, over the years, knowingly monitored nicotine levels in a bid to keep smokers hooked.

Perhaps the best evidence that nicotine is a crucial component of the cigarette business is the dismal failure of a virtually nicotine-free cigarette from Philip Morris called Next. The company spent more than $300 million to develop Next, but the nicotine-free cigarette flopped in test markets.[26] As M.A.H. Russell wrote in a 1974 article entitled "The Smoking Habit and Its Classification": "There is little doubt that if it were not for the nicotine in tobacco smoke, people would be little more inclined to smoke than they are to blow bubbles or to light sparklers."[27]

But while nicotine gets the most attention for its role in hooking smokers, there are some far nastier and deadlier compounds in the cigarette. Indeed, although a 1989 Surgeon General's report says that nicotine can be a factor in heart disease and pregnancy problems, most scientists say that other components of cigarettes have even greater health consequences. Tar, for example, is one of the major culprits because it delivers numerous carcinogenic substances throughout the body. Tar is a solid particle of partially burned tobacco that enters the body when a smoker inhales. So far, about 4,000 different compounds have been identified in cigarette smoke, including carbon monoxide.

An article in the medical journal *Cancer Research* in 1953 by doctors at Memorial Sloan-Kettering Cancer Center in New York focused on the effects of tar. The researchers discovered that smoke condensate, when painted on the skin of mice, produced tumors in 44 percent of the animals. They imagined that the smoke was doing far worse things to the insides of the human lung. But tar, unlike nicotine, isn't a crucial component of cigarettes. Sensing popular demand for lower-tar cigarettes, cigarette manufacturers began adding filters to cigarettes to reduce the amount of tar inhaled by smokers. Research shows, however, that the filters don't do much in terms of reducing the actual tar that a smoker inhales. The reason: Tar levels aren't determined by the actual ingredients of the cigarettes but by the way the smoker puffs, that is, how long the smoker draws on the cigarette and how deeply he or she inhales the smoke. One study even found that many smokers inadvertently block the little holes in the sides of a cigarette aimed at reducing the amount of smoke the smoker inhales. So most smokers of low-tar cigarettes probably aren't getting less tar in the end.

Nonetheless, the filter gives a neat appearance to the cigarette, and it also keeps the end from getting soggy and shedding tobacco bits on a smoker's lips and mouth. In addition, filters proved to be a useful divergence in the tobacco debate. By shifting health concerns to tar levels (something tobacco companies could do something about), cigarette makers were able to steer the debate away from nicotine, the essential ingredient the manufacturers and smokers couldn't do without. "If the nicotine delivery is reduced below a threshold satisfaction level, then surely smokers will question more readily why they are indulging in an expensive habit," wrote one senior BAT scientist in 1976. He recommended that BAT attempt to frame the public debate about cigarettes to focus on the tar. "It is advocated that every opportunity is taken to separate tar and nicotine in the minds of consumers and legislators," he wrote.[28]

The strategy is typical of the cigarette industry, which closely monitors every stage of cigarette production, from the plants the industry uses to the flavors and additives it blends with the leaf. Even the way the tightness of the cigarette paper affects the burn rate and the impact of store counter displays on cigarette purchases are scrutinized to guarantee that smokers keep coming back for more. In the transformation of the tobacco plant from seed to smoke, nothing is left to chance.

4.

Selling Smoke:
Marketing and Advertising

*"No particular ability is required to sell meat or
flour or shoes. . . . But to sell a man something he doesn't even
know he wants is a very different thing."*
—U.S. TOBACCO JOURNAL

"They got lips. We want 'em."
—UNIDENTIFIED RJR EXECUTIVE

Creative Fires

How do you convince millions of men and women every day to
buy something they really don't need? That has been the plight of
the tobacco industry since the earliest days of the cigarette and the
single biggest reason the cigarette has emerged as perhaps the
quintessential advertised product in the annals of modern marketing. Tobacco has always been a luxury, an indulgent pleasure,
that man could clearly do without. As tobacco historian Gerard
Petrone wrote in *Tobacco Advertising: The Great Seduction*, tobacco merchants have "a driving need . . . to create a demand where
none had existed before."[1]

Creating that need isn't cheap. When a smoker puts his or her money on the counter to buy a pack of cigarettes, about 15 percent of the price is used by cigarette makers to advertise and promote their brands. Even among consumer products companies, who tend to be the world's biggest advertisers, this is a startlingly high percentage. At Procter & Gamble Co., for instance, which regularly tops the list of the world's biggest advertisers, advertising and promotion costs are equal to about 10 percent of company sales. Athletic shoe companies, including big advertisers like Nike Corp., spend an average of about 9 percent. General Motors, another big advertiser, spends the equivalent of 2 percent of sales on advertising.[2]

There are three key reasons why cigarette companies spend billions promoting their brands. The first, and perhaps most important to the future of the industry, is to entice new smokers, no small task since people don't naturally crave nicotine. Once cigarette makers have wooed new smokers, advertising helps them instill brand loyalty and keep them smoking. Finally, at a time when smoking rates are relatively flat or declining in developed markets such as the United States and Europe, advertising is the primary way cigarette companies steal market share from competitors by creating image-oriented ads and promotional gimmicks that convince smokers to switch brands.

Wooing new smokers (the tobacco industry refers to them as "pre-smokers") is perhaps the most challenging task facing the cigarette industry, especially given the widespread antitobacco campaigning so prevalent in the United States and Europe and which has even begun to percolate in developing nations. In addition, by now most people know smoking can cause disease and even death. Compounding the problem is the fact that there's no natural market for cigarettes and no compelling need for nonsmokers to buy them. Compare cigarettes to other consumer products, such as laundry detergent and shampoo. Most people in the developed world consider clean clothes and clean hair a necessity, for both aesthetic and personal health reasons. Products like Coca-Cola or Gatorade have a natural appeal among thirsty consumers, while disposable diapers and razors, though not necessary for survival, certainly have become essential to modern living. So although companies like Coca-Cola and Procter & Gamble do advertise to promote their brands as better than a competitor's, they are one step ahead of the cigarette industry because they don't have to convince consumers to *begin* washing their clothes, quenching their thirst, or shaving their beards.

But what about life's other little luxuries like candy bars, chewing gum, fast-food hamburgers, or a glass of wine? To be sure, makers of fattening foods and alcoholic beverages do face similar challenges, and, like cigarette makers, often rely more on image than substance to woo new users. But while many people have a natural craving for sweets and fatty foods, nobody naturally craves nicotine. And eating, chewing, and drinking do come more naturally than setting fire to brown leaves and inhaling.

So how do you get that first cigarette into the hands of a nonsmoker? Cigarette makers figured out early on that by using aspirational images of independent women, free-spirited men, and cuddly cartoon characters, they could win new smokers—young men, women, teens, and consumers abroad—to the fold.

Nowhere has this strategy been more evident than in an illuminating 1972 in-house memo from Claude Teague, assistant chief in research and development at R.J. Reynolds. In the memo, Teague discusses the factors that induce "a pre-smoker or non-smoker" to become a "habituated smoker." That smoker, Teague writes, doesn't "start to smoke to satisfy a non-existent craving for nicotine."

> *Rather, he appears to start to smoke for purely psychological reasons—to emulate a valued image, to conform, to experiment, to defy, to be daring, to have something to do with his hands, and the like. Only after experiencing smoking for some*

period of time do the physiological "satisfactions" and habitua-
tion become apparent and needed. Indeed, the first smoking
experiences are often unpleasant until a tolerance for nicotine
has been developed. This leaves us, then, in the position of
attempting to design and promote the same product to two dif-
ferent types of market with two different sets of motivations,
needs and expectations. . . .

If we are to attract the non-smoker or pre-smoker, there is
nothing in this type of product that he would currently under-
stand or desire. We have deliberately played down the role of
nicotine, hence the non-smoker has little or no knowledge of
what satisfactions it may offer him and no desire to try it.
Instead, we somehow must convince him with wholly irra-
tional reasons that he should try smoking, in the hope that he
will for himself then discover the real "satisfactions" obtain-
able.[3]

Despite Teague's insights, cigarette makers deny that they target nonsmokers and say their sole reason for advertising is to instill
brand loyalty and steal smokers away from competing brands.
"Not only do we not market toward teens, but advertising and
promotion is not effective in influencing people to smoke," a
Philip Morris spokesman told the *Los Angeles Times* in 1994. "It
can help people choose a brand if they already smoke, and it can
enhance brand recognition."[4]

To be sure, instilling brand loyalty and stealing smokers away
from competing brands is crucial to a cigarette company's success,
especially considering that the pool of existing smokers is declining
in many countries. And it is becoming increasingly difficult for cigarette makers to counter the antismoking efforts that keep many
young people from starting the habit. But history has shown that
cigarette makers, with the right advertising mix and gimmickry,
can steal customers. Consider that at one time the most popular
cigarette in the United States was Lucky Strike. By 1950, Camel

FIGURE 12:
World's Most Popular Cigarette Brands

BRAND AND MANUFACTURER	VOLUME SALES	WORLD MARKET SHARE
Marlboro (Philip Morris)	476 billion	9.4%
Mild Seven (Japan Tobacco)	135 billion	2.7%
L&M (Philip Morris)	91 billion	1.8%
Winston (R.J. Reynolds)	7.1 billion	1.4%
Camel (R.J. Reynolds)	67 billion	1.3%

SOURCE: Euromonitor.

had taken over the top spot, but Winston was the market leader in 1970. By 1990 Marlboro, boosted by the rugged Marlboro cowboy, was the country's most popular cigarette. [See Fig. 12]

The history of cigarette advertising is closely intertwined with the evolution of advertising in general. Modern methods of advertising and promotion were spawned by the prosperity of the Industrial Revolution in the nineteenth century. Men and women had money to spend and manufacturers had goods to sell.

Only those companies that could distinguish their goods from the surfeit of new competing products would succeed. The further limits of the tobacco business—the challenge of selling a man "something he doesn't know he wants"—sparked the creative fires of the cigarette merchants. They used enticing imagery, testimonials, and giveaways to distinguish their products, and they quickly spotted the powerful potential of mass marketing with the emergence of radio and television. "Tobacco manufacturers, imbued with long-range vision and an innate power of persuasion, pioneered selling techniques that literally stood conventional advertising on its ear and revolutionized the American way of doing business," writes Petrone, the advertising historian. "They were good at what they did."[5]

Cigarette Trading Cards
(© Bettmann/Corbis)

Cigarette advertising has its origins in the earliest days of the commercial tobacco business, when tobacconists began touting the virtues of their own blends. In the early eighteenth century, tobacco merchants placed ads in newspapers in the form of a riddle—the answer could only be learned by a trip to the tobacco shop. Tobacconists handed out trading cards and included collectible metal tags in bags of tobacco that could later be redeemed for merchandise.

Some of the earliest advertising of tobacco was initiated by the Bull Durham tobacco brand of North Carolina. The trademark owner, John Green, borrowed the bull logo from a jar of Colman's mustard. The brand became popular after Civil War soldiers plundered the factory and pocketed the special smoking tobacco. After the war, the factory was inundated with letters from soldiers who wanted more of the delicious smoke—although this time they were willing to buy it. The firm, later named Blackwell Co., plastered the bull logo on billboards and promoted the brand with endorsements from prominent politicians, clergymen, and even the British poet laureate Alfred Lord Tennyson. In the early 1880s, the firm is said to have spent $150,000 advertising in newspapers and another $60,000 on clocks that were given away as premiums. The firm's president, Julian S. Carr, was among the first of the tobacco marketers to spot the powerful potential of the advertisement. "As long as I have a dollar to spare," said Carr, "I will invest it in advertising."[6]

Another popular enticement of the time was the cigarette trading card, America's first major advertising medium. Allen & Gintner of Richmond and Buck Duke of Durham included the cards in cigarette packs. The cards, which included pictures of actresses, sultry models, rare animals, and war heroes, quickly became collectibles.

But it was the launch of Camels in 1913 that revolutionized cigarette advertising. A series of teaser ads piqued the interest of consumers. One ad said simply: "The Camels are Coming!" Another promised: "Camels! Tomorrow there will be more Camels in this town than in all Asia and Africa combined!"[7]

The campaign was unique because the manufacturer, Reynolds, opted to put all of its marketing and advertising muscle behind just one brand at a time when big cigarette companies were promoting a variety of brands from their stable of products. The success of the Camels campaign prompted competitors to copy the strategy. American Tobacco Co. searched through its portfolio of brands and chose Lucky Strike, redesigning the package with a bull's-eye circle. When company president George Washington Hill heard someone explain that the heat used to make cigarettes was similar to that used in cooking, he came up with the appetizing slogan: "Lucky Strike. It's Toasted." The earliest ads showed a piece of toast with a fork through it. Although the heating process used to make Luckies was the same used by

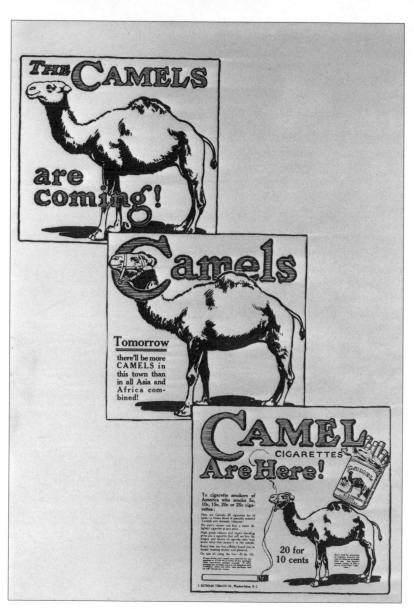

Early Camel Cigarette Advertisement

(© Bettmann/Corbis)

all tobacco manufacturers of the day, the company promoted the feature as "the most modern step in cigarette manufacturing," and even claimed that it made the cigarette "mild" and "less irritating."[8] One promotion called on doctors to try Lucky Strikes—those who agreed they were less irritating were given several free cartons. The result was an ad that proclaimed: "20,679 Physicians say Luckies are Less Irritating."

It quickly became clear that the focused advertising and fierce competition among manufacturers was a boon to cigarette sales. Per capita consumption, which had been 173 cigarettes in 1911, surged to 727 by 1919.[9] The heyday of modern cigarette advertising began in the 1920s. It was as if the rise in cigarette consumption had ignited the imaginations of the tobacco ad men, who managed to link smoking with everything from weight loss to "throat protection." One ad in 1938 for Camels told readers: "High-tension times are hard on nerves," and included testimonials from an actress and a Western Union telegrapher who smoked Camels to relax. "Let up—Light up a Camel. Smokers find Camel's Costlier Tobaccos are Soothing to the Nerves." Another ad for Chesterfields showed a popular actor named Ronald Reagan, with the endorsement, "My cigarette is the mild cigarette."[10]

Although FTC officials began cracking down on claims that cigarettes were mild or less irritating, the tone for cigarette advertising had been set. Clearly, cigarette makers sensed the potential health toll cigarettes could take, and as a result concocted healthy images and endorsements to preempt those fears. Indeed, a 1988 study by Richard W. Pollay, marketing professor at the University of British Columbia, found that among 567 cigarette ads appearing between 1938 and 1983, 60 percent pushed a "healthiness" message by using health claims, medical endorsements, exuberant models, and clean and pure outdoor scenes like mountains and forests.[11]

In the early 1920s, cigarette makers also discovered that

advertising was a way to tap into that elusive half of the population that hadn't yet taken up the smoking habit: women. At the time, although smoking was an acceptable pastime for men, it was still relatively taboo for women.

In 1927, Lucky Strike began using testimonials from opera stars and other women, promising "No throat irritation—no cough." But it was on a ride home from work that American Tobacco president George Washington Hill reportedly got the inspiration for the Lucky Strike campaign that would forever change the way cigarettes were marketed to women. He was sitting in his car at 110th Street and Fifth Avenue in New York when he noticed an overweight woman chewing gum. A taxicab rolled by and Hill's wandering eye noticed a slim young woman riding in the cab. His view was such that he noticed her short skirt and that she was smoking a cigarette through a long, slim cigarette holder. "Right then and there it hit me," recounted Hill. "There was the . . . lady that was stout and chewing (gum), and there was the young girl that was slim and smoking a cigarette."

The new slogan: "Reach for a Lucky Instead of a Sweet." Sales increased threefold in just 12 months.[12]

The ad campaign outraged candy manufacturers, and the Federal Trade Commission told Hill that he couldn't advertise cigarettes as a weight-loss device, so the slogan was changed to "Reach for a Lucky Instead." Even so, new ads for Lucky Strikes continued to push the message of smoking as an appetite suppressant by showing attractive people in various poses, with silhouettes of overweight shadows behind them. One ad in 1929 warned: "Avoid that Future Shadow," and showed the profile of a double-chinned shadow behind a woman's slim profile. "When Tempted, Reach for a Lucky."

A Lucky Strike ad of 1932 featured actress Jean Harlow. "She's mischievous, restless and 20, weighs 112 pounds." The ad included a testimonial from the actress herself. "I've tried all cigarettes and there's none so good as Luckies. And incidentally I'm careful

Early Advertisement for Lucky Strike
(© Bettmann/Corbis)

in my choice of cigarettes. I have to be because of my throat. Put me down as one who always reaches for a Lucky."[13]

Despite growing sales, smoking remained taboo for most women. But Edward Bernays, a budding public relations guru hired by Hill, would quickly change that. Bernays, a nephew of the psychoanalyst Sigmund Freud, is widely viewed as the father of public relations, and, much to his chagrin, his book *Propaganda* was extolled for its insights by no less than Adolf Hitler.

Bernays's first foray into shaping public opinion had nothing to do with smoking but involved his support for a controversial play, *Damaged Goods*, which dealt with syphilis. Bernays, who after graduating from Cornell in 1913 began his career as a journalist, was editing a medical magazine and wrote to the play's producer to offer the backing of his medical journal, but he quickly became immersed in publicizing the play. At the time, sex, let alone a sexually transmitted disease, wasn't discussed in public so it was questionable whether *Damaged Goods* would ever be performed. But Bernays found a way to make it happen. He formed a special committee that had no obvious connection to *Damaged Goods* to educate the public about venereal diseases and enlisted the support of wealthy New Yorkers to the educational campaign. The plan worked, and *Damaged Goods* received rave reviews in the press.

"While most publicists of the day understood their job as merely handling press releases to reporters or staging ritualized press conferences, Bernays's instinct was to operate more clandestinely, behind the scenes, invisibly staging events or 'circumstances' that the press would—out of habit—consider newsworthy," writes Stuart Ewen in *PR! A Social History of Spin*.[14]

Bernays's early experience spinning New Yorkers about sex and disease is significant because it so strongly influenced the methods he would later use to shape the cigarette industry and the people who smoked its products. He once explained that in promoting a product like bacon, the traditional publicist would take out ads telling people to eat more bacon because it's cheap and tastes good. But a more effective publicity campaign doesn't focus on a product's own attributes but is rooted in the "principles of mass psychology." In other words, Bernays knew the public's eating habits were heavily influenced by physicians, so a successful bacon campaign would convince doctors to tout the benefits of bacon, and consumer acceptance would quickly follow.[15]

Bernays understood, perhaps better than anyone of his time, how corporations could tap into the whims of the masses. As he explained in *Propaganda*:

> *The group mind does not think in the strict sense of the word. In place of thoughts it has impulses, habits and emotions. In making up its mind, its first impulse is usually to follow the example of a trusted leader. This is one of the most firmly established principles of mass psychology.*[16]

As a result, when Hill asked Bernays for advice in promoting cigarettes, the publicity guru literally put smoking on the couch. In 1929, Bernays consulted with psychoanalyst A. A. Brill for advice on how to convince women to start smoking. Brill told him:

Women Bathers Lighting a Cigarette
(© Hulton-Deutsch Collection/Corbis)

*Some women regard cigarettes as symbols of freedom.
Smoking is a sublimation of oral eroticism; holding a cigarette
in the mouth excites the oral zone. It is perfectly normal for
women to want to smoke cigarettes. Further the first women
who smoked probably had an excess of masculine components
and adopted the habit as a masculine act. But today the eman-
cipation of women has suppressed many of the feminine desires.
More women now do the same work as men do. . . . Cigarettes,
which are equated with men, become torches of freedom.*[17]

As a result of the consultation, Bernays didn't recommend
that cigarette advertising tell women they would enjoy smoking. Instead, he tapped into the social consciousness of women

yearning for independence and equality. At a time when women rarely smoked in public, Bernays arranged for 19 pretty debutantes to march up Fifth Avenue in New York's 1929 Easter Parade while smoking cigarettes. The women waved their cigarettes, proclaiming them "torches of liberty," an image that was captured by photographers and displayed in newspapers around the world. The strategy worked. By 1931, women accounted for 14 percent of U.S. tobacco consumption, up from just 5 percent in 1924.[18]

Bernays became a master of the staged publicity stunt on behalf of the tobacco industry. In 1934, when Lucky Strike sales faltered, research suggested that it was because the brand's green package clashed with ladies' clothes. In a bid to make a green pack of Lucky Strikes a more fashionable accessory, Bernays persuaded a silk maker to make green the color of the season. He then convinced a New York socialite to sponsor a Green Ball, paid for with $25,000 from American Tobacco Co., where women arrived wearing green gowns.

The surge in the number of women smokers wasn't without controversy. In 1938, *Reader's Digest* remarked on the new affront to manners. "Women have brushed aside all traditions of courtesy and consideration regarding smoking. Men respect a few conventions, but who has ever heard a woman asking permission to smoke?"[19]

One drawback of the advertising binge was that it dramatically raised the profile of the cigarette makers. And as smoking rates continued to climb—jumping from 665 cigarettes per capita in 1920 to 1,485 in 1930[20]—so did attention from public health officials, who were just beginning to suspect cigarettes as the culprit behind a startling rise in lung cancer. But as has so often proved the case with the cigarette industry, manufacturers found a way to use this bit of gloom and doom to their advantage. A handful of companies launched cigarettes with filter tips and created advertising that would play on smokers' growing health

Winston Cigarettes on the Production Line
(© Farrell Grehan/Corbis)

worries. In 1952, Lorillard launched its Kent filter, touting it as "the greatest health protection in cigarette history." Liggett's L&M filter brand was "just what the doctor ordered."[1]

Executives at Reynolds didn't think it was such a good idea to remind smokers of the potential dangers of the habit. So they decided to focus on the flaws of most filter cigarettes—that the filter worked too well and took out most of the flavor. The company launched Winston in 1954 with the slogan, "Winston tastes good—like a cigarette should."[21]

Filter cigarettes got off to a slow start—by 1954 filters accounted for only about 10 percent of industry sales. But in one of the great ironies of the cigarette business, the health concerns that prompted the development of the filter tip also spurred the re-launch and re-packaging of another brand, Marlboro. Marlboro developed such a powerful and enticing brand image that it would eventually steamroll its competitors and win scores of new smokers to its ranks, making it the scourge of antismoking activists.

Marlboro Is for Girls

The story of Marlboro's success illustrates just how malleable a product's image is and how well the cigarette makers have grown to understand the power of imagery in influencing consumer buying habits.

By 1954, Philip Morris was in a slump. Sales of Philip Morris cigarettes fell 13 percent that year,[22] and rival R.J. Reynolds was winning smokers with its new Winston brand, a filter cigarette with a stronger flavor than most filter brands.

Philip Morris knew it needed to introduce its own filter brand to compete, and it chose Marlboro, a small brand that until then had been promoted as a mild smoke primarily for women. "Mild as May" read one ad, which showed a woman's well-manicured hand with a long black cigarette holder. "Tried them yet? . . . They lend an added charm to smoking."[23] Marlboro's even had a "rosy" tip to hide women's lipstick stains.

To start the makeover, Philip Morris revamped the product package after researchers told them a red package would convey a stronger flavor. To stand out, the company also opted for a new, boxlike cigarette container with a hinged top. But Philip Morris's executive vice president of marketing, Joseph F. Cullman III, decided the brand needed more than just a packaging makeover. It desperately needed a new, more masculine image that would win male smokers without putting off women. It also needed to convince smokers that, even with the filter, the flavor was strong and pleasurable. At the same time, the company couldn't boast too strong a flavor for fear of scaring off new smokers, who would beg off a cigarette if they thought it sounded too harsh.

It was a tall order. Cullman called on the Chicago ad agency Leo Burnett, which had a growing reputation as a hot creative shop, probably best known for the Jolly Green Giant campaign.

"We talked with Leo for several hours at his office, describing the marketing problem we had," said Cullman, as quoted in *Star Reacher*, a history of the Leo Burnett ad agency. "Our Marlboro brand—a cigarette designed and marketed to women with its ivory and rose tips—had been around for a good many years as a very high-grade brand at a premium price. Now we wanted to change the image of Marlboro. . . . "[24]

Burnett and several agency executives brainstormed at Burnett's farm for a weekend. A *Life* magazine cover showing a cowboy smoking a cigarette reportedly caught Burnett's eye. "Do you know anything more masculine than a cowboy?" he told his colleagues.

The following Monday, Burnett was ready to pitch his idea to executives at Philip Morris. He unveiled an ad featuring a rugged, unshaven cowboy smoking a cigarette. The headline on the ad was simple: "New From Philip Morris." And the copy continued at the bottom corner of the page: "You get a lot to like. Filter, flavor, flip-top box." Burnett also suggested that the red stripes on the top of the package be changed to solid red, because he thought it looked stronger and more masculine. And he insisted that the lower-case M in Marlboro designed by Philip Morris packaging consultants instead be capitalized for the simple reason that "a brand must have a capital letter at the beginning."[25]

The pitch won Leo Burnett the account. Burnett outlined the campaign strategy in a letter dated January 7, 1955, that explained why the ads included pictures of cowboys and rugged-looking men with tattoos.

> *You'll notice all these advertisements feature men and you may wonder about that. This is why. Research by the Elmo Roper organization shows that many people think of filter cigarettes as a woman's smoke. . . . This is not the personality we want for the New Marlboro. . . .*

The Marlboro Man

(© The Purcell Team/Corbis)

*The cowboy is an almost universal symbol of admired mas-
culinity. The man in the evening suit has a tattoo on his wrist. We
think this will not only startle the reader into looking at the ad and
cause him to remember it, but that it will say to many men that
here is a successful man who used to work with his hands. To many
women, we believe it will suggest a romantic past.*

*This almost sounds as though Dr. Freud were on our Plans
Board. He isn't. We've been guided by research and old-fashioned horse sense.*[26]

The campaign got off to a strong start, propelling the new filter Marlboro to fourth place among 11 filter brands. But by the
1960s, Marlboro ran into some new problems. Rival salesmen had
begun spreading rumors that the super-strong Marlboro had been
banned from military bases and prohibited in some states. It wasn't
true, but to counter the attack, Marlboro ads in 1961 reminded
smokers: "Wherever you travel this summer from the Klondike to
Key West, in any state in every state, you're in Marlboro Country."[27]

Although it was born out of a crisis, the campaign actually
helped complete Marlboro's makeover. Marlboro was no longer
just a cigarette, but a lifestyle, a smoke for the rugged individual-
ist who longed for simpler times and the chance to escape to the
wide-open spaces of Marlboro Country.

The earliest ads for the new Marlboro featured both cowboys
and men with tattoos and even some executives from Philip
Morris and Leo Burnett, but market researchers discovered that
sales noticeably quickened when the cowboy ads appeared. Their
own research found that the cowboy appealed to younger male
smokers, who were looking for ways to show their independence.

The campaign didn't win Marlboro market leadership
overnight, but it slowly and steadily picked up smokers, especially
new smokers. By 1972, the Marlboro cowboy had rounded up
enough new and existing smokers to make it the market leader. It
has remained so ever since.

Although clever ad campaigns featuring images like the Marlboro man and testimonials from actresses spurred cigarette sales, it was the advent of broadcast radio and television that allowed cigarette marketers to spread their smoking message to the masses.

The 1930s marked the arrival of broadcast advertising, and by 1940 the leading companies were spending more than half of their ad budgets on radio advertisements. The cigarette makers discovered a whole new way to deliver their message through sponsorship of radio programs—a method the companies quickly discovered gave their products a stronger ring of credibility with consumers. So radio listeners heard the Lucky Strike "Hit Parade" while Philip Morris sponsored a weekly music variety show. It was on that variety show that Philip Morris's first pitchman, Johnny Roventini, made his famous debut, shouting out "Call for Philip Morris!"

By 1946, when radio broadcasting was at its peak, the tobacco companies were mulling a new, if untested, medium: television. At the time, the United States had just 6,000 sets, but that number would balloon to 100,000 in 1947.[28] By 1948, Philip Morris was pushing ads on television, sponsoring feel-good shows such as *Candid Camera* and *This Is Your Life*. In 1951, the company paid $19,000 per episode to sponsor a show about a wacky redhead named Lucy and her Cuban bandleader husband, Ricky Ricardo. The *I Love Lucy* show quickly became the top-ranked television program. In several episodes, Lucy and Ricky even smoked on screen.[29]

But it wasn't just paid advertising that prompted cigarettes to appear on television. On November 18, 1951, Edward R. Murrow began his first broadcast of *See It Now*, the first documentary series in television history. He was unsure about the medium and felt more comfortable on the radio. "This is an old team trying to learn a new trade," he said, gazing out toward his viewers through a swirl of his own trademark cigarette smoke.[30]

Like every consumer products advertiser swarming to the new medium, cigarette makers grabbed as much television advertising time as possible. But while the advertising helped the companies peddle their brands, it further raised the industry's profile at a time when the public health community was warning about the ravages of cigarette smoking. By the 1960s, tobacco companies were spending 80 percent of their advertising budgets on television. At the time, the Federal Trade Commission found that every household in the United States with a television was being exposed to 800 cigarette commercials a year, and it proposed banning cigarette advertising on television.[31]

Both the broadcast and tobacco industries fought the proposal, but worries about the risk of smoking had begun to permeate the American consciousness. Evidence was mounting about the risks associated with smoking, and cigarette companies realized the odds were against them. The industry, fearful that public opinion was shifting quickly and that Congress could propose even more onerous legislation, did a prompt about-face. The companies volunteered to get out of television all together, but on the condition that new cigarette warning labels wouldn't mention the ugly C-word—cancer.

They struck a deal with Congress, and on December 31, 1970, the last cigarette ad appeared on television. It was a 90-second Marlboro commercial that aired at 11:58:30 and showed a group of Marlboro cowboys galloping off into the sunset.[32]

While the loss of television advertising seemed like a major setback to the industry, the cigarette companies saw opportunity. After all, tobacco ads had been banned from television in Britain in 1965, and the following year consumption there had surged by 6 billion cigarettes.[33] Cigarette makers had simply pushed their ad dollars into other forms of promotions, such as coupon and gift schemes that offered smokers free gifts for collecting a certain number of coupons from cigarette packs.

In 1976, five years after the U.S. television advertising ban, it was clear that the decision to give up the medium was far from a setback for the industry. "The reduction in cigarette advertising seems to have made the industry stronger economically," wrote Ernest Pepples, Brown & Williamson's senior vice president and general counsel in 1976. "Profits have increased. The ban on television and other broadcast advertising does not seem to have reduced consumption. The concomitant reduction in the number of anti-cigarette commercials is considered to be a severe loss in the effort to keep public concern and awareness of the controversy at a fever pitch."[34]

While advertising campaigns like the Marlboro cowboy advanced the cause of the cigarette, the tobacco industry also received an unintentional assist from Hollywood. During the 1930s and 1940s, actors, directors, and writers discovered the cigarette as prop. The 1933 film *Roberta* features one of the most famous smoking moments in Hollywood as wafts of smoke surround Irene Dunne while she sings, "When a lovely flame dies, smoke gets in your eyes." Marlene Dietrich, Carole Lombard, Jean Harlow, and Claudette Colbert smoked up the screens, while Lauren Bacall, in the 1944 film *To Have and Have Not,* oozed sex appeal when she asked the simple question, "Anybody got a match?" Smoking could convey sophistication (Audrey Hepburn as Holly Golightly puffed on a cigarette holder in *Breakfast at Tiffany's*); strength and isolation (Humphrey Bogart in *Casablanca*); and tawdriness (Diane Keaton as the good-girl teacher gone bad in *Looking for Mr. Goodbar*).

But while smoking on the silver screen at first simply reflected the fashion of the times and the filmmakers' artistic designs, the tobacco companies—like other makers of consumer goods—eventually realized that the movies could be used as a powerful medium to promote their brands, especially after they ceded television advertising. Although it's never been clear how much product

Marlene Dietrich

placement in movies the tobacco companies engaged in, several documents have surfaced to show the practice was pervasive. The document trail begins in 1979, although smoking critics believe the practice began years earlier.[35]

A particularly illuminating exchange of documents involves a discussion among Brown & Williamson executives about their dissatisfaction with Associated Film Promotion (AFP), the firm the company had hired to "place" its cigarette brands in various movies. The goal was to have actors smoking B&W brands and to have the camera sweep by posters or trucks or billboards carrying B&W logos. According to *The Cigarette Papers*, which analyzes reams of once-secret B&W documents, the company paid $965,500 to AFP from 1979 through 1983 for movie placements and retainer fees.[36]

Although B&W wasn't happy with the display its products were getting, the exchange of memos between B&W executives shows the extent to which B&W, the company's competitors, and even moviemakers and actors, were using product placement of cigarettes in films.

In a letter to AFP in 1983, actor Sylvester Stallone made it clear that smoking in his films was a matter of financial, not artistic, need. "I guarantee that I will use Brown & Williamson tobacco products in no less than five feature films. It is my understanding that Brown & Williamson will pay a fee of $500,000."[37]

In response, AFP senior vice president James F. Ripkin summarized the terms of the deal. Among other things, it was clear that Stallone would personally use B&W cigarettes in several roles except in *Rocky IV*. Rocky Balboa, Stallone's character, wasn't a smoker, but the company noted that B&W brands would be smoked by other characters, and B&W signs and ads could appear, possibly in or around the boxing ring. (B&W's contract with AFP ended before all the films were made.)

A later audit of B&W's payments to AFP showed that B&W also had paid to place its cigarette brands in such movies as *Body*

Heat, First Blood, Jinxed, Only When I Laugh, Nine to Five, and *Never Say Never Again*, among others. Documents show that the practices also involved a considerable amount of perquisites provided by the tobacco company for the individuals making the movies, including $7,170 worth of jewelry for Sean Connery while making *Never Say Never Again*, a $42,000 car for Paul Newman in *Harry & Son*, and an $80,000 horse for Sylvester Stallone. (A *Los Angeles Times* investigation found that many of the gifts never reached the stars.) All-in-all, AFP reportedly attempted to place B&W cigarettes in 150 movies and succeeded in getting them to show up in 22 films and one television show, *The A-Team*.[38]

B&W wasn't the only cigarette maker engaging in the practice. In 1984, American Tobacco Co. paid $5,000 and provided other props to place Lucky Strike in *Beverly Hills Cop*. Liggett & Myers paid $30,000 for its Eve cigarettes to appear in the movie *Supergirl*. The company responded to a direct solicitation from the movie's production company that compared the opportunity to the similar placement of Marlboro cigarettes in *Superman II*.

> *Audiences everywhere will recall watching the titanic battle over Metropolis between Superman and the Arch Villains, which occurred in front of gigantic Coca-Cola and Cutty Sark signs, and will be able to tell you that a truck bearing a prominent Marlboro logo played an important role in the sequence. The advertising opportunities on (Supergirl's) Midvale Street will be equally as memorable.*
>
> *In addition to the outdoor billboard advertisements, exposure can be provided on storefronts, bus shelters, neon signs and trade vehicles. We are also offering a variety of promotional and premium opportunities, and are developing plans for advertiser tie-in promotions. . . .* [39]

A Congressional hearing in 1989 revealed that Philip Morris paid $42,500 in 1979 to place Marlboro cigarettes in *Superman II*, paid $350,000 for the Lark brand to show up in *License to Kill*, a James Bond movie, and that the company in 1987 and 1988 provided free cigarettes and other props for 56 different films.[40] A B&W memo speculates that Philip Morris paid as much as $200,000 for Marlboro to appear in *Apocalypse Now*. Martin Sheen smokes Marlboro throughout the movie, but B&W executive J.M. Coleman is critical of the deal. "This placement is not worth $200M because the actual logo is not seen, and because of the setting, they were not able to use any other product identification (i.e. billboard, cab top)," he wrote. "This movie is a Marlboro commercial only to people in our industry because we know the pack and the cigarette brand even when the pack is not shown—but to an ordinary person, the pack/cigarette shots are not that intrusive."[41]

B&W eventually canceled its dealings with AFP because the company felt it wasn't getting its money's worth. "The use of any cigarette by a movie hero advertises all cigarettes. So let the competitors help advertise our brands in this way," wrote Ernest Pepples, B&W's senior vice president and general counsel. He noted that continuing with product placement was "foolish" for both "business and political reasons."[42]

Today, tobacco companies have voluntarily agreed to stop using product placement in movies, but the issue of smoking in films remains controversial. Tobacco critics, citing actors such as John Travolta, Winona Ryder, and Julia Roberts, among others, say Hollywood continues to glorify smoking, particularly among young people. A study by the University of California—San Francisco found that in the mid 1990s, smoking among lead actors occurred at four times the rate of smoking among the population at large.[43]

Nonetheless, cigarettes on the silver screen and the small screen have indelibly shaped the smoking habits of the current generation. Even though cigarette marketers no longer advertise on television or place their products in Hollywood movies, both mediums have served to enhance and solidify the glamorous image of smoking and continue to influence the images and methods tobacco companies use to market their products around the world today.

Tomorrow's Smokers

While cigarette makers have long claimed their advertising efforts are aimed only at convincing existing smokers to switch brands, advertising has proven to be an effective method for replenishing the ranks of smokers. After all, the World Health Organization estimates that 3.5 million people die each year of smoking-related ailments. A study in 1986 by tobacco opponents found that, based on the fact that a majority of smokers start the habit by the age of 13, about 5,000 children and teenagers need to start smoking each day to maintain the current size of the smoking population.[44]

Despite the industry's claims to the contrary, cigarette makers years ago set their sights on winning new smokers, according to a 1950 article in the *U.S. Tobacco Journal.* "A massive potential market still exists among women and young adults, cigarette industry leaders agreed, acknowledging that recruitment of these millions of prospective smokers comprises the major objective for the immediate future and on a long term basis as well."[45]

Women were among the earliest targets in the effort to recruit new smokers. Following the efforts of Edward Bernays, women had taken up smoking in droves. But most of the brands on the market were originally targeted at men. So in 1967 Philip Morris launched a cigarette designed for and aimed specifically at women—Virginia Slims. The cigarettes were long and slim and the ad campaign from Leo Burnett told women: "You've come a long way baby, to get to where you've got today." A year later, American Brands rolled out Silva Thins. [See Fig. 13]

"I knew thinness was a quality worth talking about," said John T. Landry, Philip Morris's marketing chief at the time. "It's an American obsession."[46]

Smoking Rates of Women vs. Men Around the World
(as a percentage of the population)

COUNTRY	WOMEN VS. MEN
Denmark	37 vs. 37
Russia	30 vs. 67
Israel	30 vs. 45
Poland	29 vs. 51
Canada	29 vs. 31
Greece	28 vs. 46
France	27 vs. 40
Great Britain	26 vs. 28
Italy	26 vs. 38
Brazil	25.4 vs. 39.9
Spain	25 vs. 48
Turkey	24 vs. 63
Sweden	24 vs. 22
United States	23.5 vs. 28.1
Argentina	23 vs. 40
Germany	21.5 vs. 36.8
Bolivia	21.4 vs. 50
Australia	21 vs. 29
Belgium	19 vs. 31
Guatemala	17.7 vs. 37.8
South Africa	17 vs. 52
Japan	14.8 vs. 59
Mexico	14.4 vs. 38.3
Dominican Republic	13.6 vs. 66.3
Philippines	8 vs. 43
China	7 vs. 61
Thailand	4 vs. 49
India	3 vs. 40
Singapore	2.7 vs. 31.9
Egypt	1 vs. 39.8

SOURCE: World Health Organization.

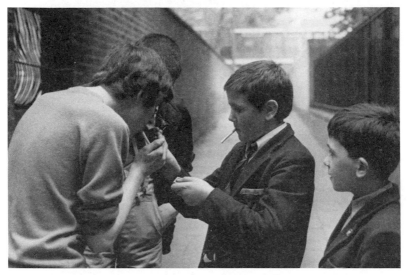

Schoolboy Smokers
(© Hulton-Deutsch Collection/Corbis)

From 1967 to 1975, sales of Virginia Slims, Silva, and Eve flourished, raking in $16 billion in sales in 1976. But while the ads were aimed at women, they proved surprisingly effective on young girls. A study by Dr. John Pierce of the University of California at San Diego found that beginning in 1967, at the time the Virginia Slims ads debuted, smoking among 11- to 17-year-old girls surged, jumping at least 35 percent and as much as 110 percent in each age group.[47]

A spate of internal industry documents shows that tobacco companies were well aware that their brands and advertising also appealed to children, and many were searching for ways to capitalize on it. In 1957, a Philip Morris executive conceded in a memo that reaching young people was expensive but much more efficient than targeting adults. "They are willing to experiment, they have more influence over others in their age group than they will later in life, and they are far more loyal to their starting brand," the memo explained.[48]

In 1969, Philip Morris noted that among smokers in the 15-

year-old age group, 15 percent of girls and 23 percent of boys smoked Marlboro.[49] In the early 1970s, B&W considered adding honey to its cigarettes because "it's a well-known fact that teenagers like sweet products."[50]

And at Reynolds, researcher Teague wrote an internal memo in 1973 entitled "Some Thoughts About New Brands of Cigarettes for the Youth Market."

> At the outset it should be said that we are presently, and I believe unfairly, constrained from directly promoting cigarettes to the youth market . . . if our company is to survive and prosper, over the long term we must get our share of the youth market. I believe it unrealistic to expect that existing brands identified with an over-thirty establishment market can ever become the "in" products with the young group. Thus we need new brands designed to be particularly attractive to the young smoker, while ideally at the same time appealing to all smokers. . . .
>
> Thus a new brand aimed at the young smoker must somehow become the "in" brand and its promotion should emphasize togetherness, belonging and group acceptance, while at the same time emphasizing individuality and "doing one's own thing." The teens and early twenties are periods of intense psychological stress, restlessness and boredom. Many socially awkward situations are encountered. . . . The fragile developing self-image of the young person needs all of the support and enhancement it can get. . . . This self-image enhancement effect has traditionally been a strong promotional theme for cigarette brands and should continue to be emphasized. . . . A careful study of current youth jargon, together with a review of currently used high school American history books and the sources for valued things might be a good start at finding a good brand name and image theme.[51]

Six months later the germ of a blockbuster idea had already

surfaced at Reynolds. A company document wonders whether "comic strip type copy might get a much higher readership among young people than any other type of copy."[52] An RJR marketing presentation dated September 30, 1974, clearly illustrated that the company was searching for ways to capture the youth market.

> First, let's take a look at the growing importance of the young adult in the cigarette market. In 1960, this young adult market, the 14-24 age group, represented 21% of the population. As seen by this chart, they will represent 27% of the population in 1975. They represent tomorrow's cigarette business. As this 14 to 25 age group matures, they will account for a key share of the total cigarette volume—for at least the next 25 years.[53]

Indeed, Reynolds was struggling for a way to slow the juggernaut of Marlboro, which research showed was dominating youth smoking. After a variety of advertising and promotion initiatives, such as the sponsorships of auto racing, Reynolds struck gold in 1988 when it reintroduced its 13-year-old Joe Camel character as a cartoon. In just three years, the brand jumped to 13 percent of the total market, up from 3 percent.[54]

At the heart of the Joe Camel campaign were giveaways—free cigarette lighters, caps, t-shirts, and jackets, all emblazoned with the cartoon logo. RJR documents show that the company focused its marketing and promotional efforts on convenience stores near high schools and colleges. In January 1990, one Florida division manager sent a memo to sales representatives asking them to study a "list of monthly accounts in your (area) that are presently doing more than 100 (cartons per week) for purposes of denoting stores that are heavily frequented by young adult shoppers. These stores can be in close proximity to colleges, high schools or areas where there are a large number of young adults frequent [*sic*] the store."[55] The manager asked the sales reps to return the list highlighting the

Joe Camel
(© *Lee Snider/Corbis*)

stores that they would classify as "young adult." RJR later said the manager had misunderstood the company's policy and that RJR salespeople did not target stores near high schools.[56]

Although Joe Camel is widely regarded as one of the most successful advertising campaigns in history, it also proved to be one of the most controversial. In 1991, a study in the *Journal of the American Medical Association* found that Joe Camel appealed far more to children than adults. As proof, the study found that children as young as six could identify Joe Camel as easily as they could Mickey Mouse.[57] But RJR was hesitant to put Old Joe out to pasture. The company's share of sales among 18 to 24 year olds had jumped to 7.9 percent, up from just 4.4 percent prior to the campaign. "Before (Joe Camel), the brand was in free-fall," one analyst told the *Economist*. "The turnaround has been miraculous."[58]

Perhaps too miraculous. In 1997, the Federal Trade Commission filed a complaint against RJR, alleging that Joe Camel violated federal laws regarding advertising to children. As a result, RJR made the public relations and legal decision to retire Old Joe in a bid to appease smoking opponents. The headline in the *New York Times* read: "Joe Camel, A Giant in Tobacco Marketing, Is Dead at 23."[59]

But while losing a popular icon like Old Joe would seem to spell disaster for RJR, the tobacco companies have proven surprisingly resilient when it comes to efforts to curb the advertising of their products. New advertising restrictions often simply force the tobacco companies to be more creative with their promotional tactics. In Britain, where tobacco advertising is heavily restricted, the cigarette makers have come up with what are widely viewed as some of the most creative and enticing ads in the world. "One of the reasons we have the most creative advertising in the world is because we've had the toughest rules for so long," says Gallaher tobacco spokesman Ian Birks.

Indeed, the U.K. rules enacted in 1975 are particularly restrictive. Ads can't be funny. Lush landscapes and scenes that depict "fresh air" aren't allowed. Blue skies must be darkened to gray. The actors depicted can't be attractive and they can't be shown smoking, exercising, or having a good time. Images that appeal to children, such as cartoon characters, are prohibited. "Basically, the ad can't be appealing," said one advertising writer.[60]

As a result, the Marlboro man is banned in the U.K.—he's too handsome. Marlboro ads in the country show bleak, desolate landscapes under the headline "Marlboro Country." Many ads don't even show cigarettes. One ad for Benson & Hedges shows someone being hypnotized by a gold watch—intended to reflect the brand's gold package. A clever campaign for Silk Cuts depicts purple silk with something sharp. One Silk Cuts ad shows a row of scissors dancing the cancan in purple silk skirts, for instance. The ads are obscure and bizarre, but they have become some of the most popular and most recognizable ads in the country.

Despite a growing number of regulations limiting tobacco advertising, tobacco companies spend about $5 billion on ciga-

Where the Advertising Dollars Go

Promotional Allowances:	$1.87 billion	(38.1%)
Coupons:	$1.35 billion	(27.5%)
Specialty Item Distribution:	$665.2 million	(13.6%)
Outdoor:	$273.7 million	(5.6%)
Point of Sale Displays:	$259 million	(5.3%)
Magazines:	$248.8 million	(5.0%)
Public Entertainment:	$110.7 million	(2.3%)
Direct Mail:	$34.6 million	(0.7%)
Transit:	$22.5 million	(0.5%)
Newspapers:	$19.1 million	(0.4%)
Samples:	$13.8 million	(0.3%)
All others:	$32.6 million	(0.7%)
	Total: $4.9 billion	

SOURCE: 1995 Federal Trade Commission Report.

rette advertising and promotion in the United States each year. Over the years, the industry has simply shifted its spending as increased scrutiny from regulators and smoking opponents has forced it out of various advertising mediums. For instance, newspapers, which accounted for 23 percent of tobacco ad spending in 1981, now reap less than 1 percent of tobacco ad dollars. Magazines, which represented 20 percent of tobacco ads in 1984, have fallen to 5 percent. Billboards and outdoor advertising, which were suspended as part of the tobacco settlement, had already fallen to 5.6 percent, down from 15.5 percent in 1983. And sampling, particularly controversial because samples can end up in the hands of underage smokers, now accounts for just 0.3 percent of spending, down from 7.9 percent in 1982. Indeed, much of the focus of the tobacco industry's ad dollars in the United States is now on promotional allowances, which give retailers financial incentives to do the cheerleading for the tobacco companies. Promotional allowances account for about 38 percent of the industry's advertising expenses.[61] [See Fig. 14]

Cigarette makers have proven particularly wily at maneuvering around a morass of advertising restrictions in several international markets, which, surprisingly, often have tougher ad restrictions than those found in the United States and parts of Europe. These markets are particularly appealing to the industry because they have significantly higher per capita smoking rates than the United States or Europe but have for years used products made by state tobacco companies that don't advertise or promote their brands. As a result, international markets are filled with millions of potential smokers, particularly women and children, who have yet to be seduced by the glamour and glitz associated with tobacco advertising and are not yet inured to Western-style advertising.

In a sign of how important advertising in international markets is to the industry, Philip Morris's ad spending outside the United States has increased by 72 percent since 1990, according to *USA Today*.[62] Although many international markets already have strict tobacco advertising bans on their books (a vestige of the days when the government wanted to protect state-run tobacco companies from competition), the bans have posed little problem for the cigarette makers. Throughout Asia, cigarette companies are skirting the ad bans with a method known as "brand stretching." Instead of promoting their cigarette brands, the tobacco companies market their trademarks on nontobacco products such as clothing, music, and even travel holidays. In Malaysia, where tobacco advertising is banned, RJR advertises its Salem Attitude clothing with the same logo and colors as Salem cigarettes. BAT promotes a Benson & Hedges bistro. In South Africa, RJR advertises Camel Party Zone CDs, and in Thailand, consumers see ads for Marlboro Classics stores. Some of the cigarette makers have even adopted the brand stretching strategy in the United States. In

1996, Philip Morris launched *Marlboro Unlimited* magazine and the Woman Thing music label, a reference to its Virginia Slims brand.

Event and sports sponsorship is also a critical component of the industry's promotional strategy abroad. In Vietnam, where tobacco advertising is banned, the Marlboro cowboy is used to promote Hollywood Night at a club. Philip Morris sponsors the China Football Association, while RJR promoted the Camel Trophy '97 jeep adventure tour in Mongolia.

Nonetheless, government agencies around the world are beginning to crack down on cigarette ad campaigns. In May 1998, the European Union voted to ban all tobacco advertising on radio, print, and television by 2001 and will stop tobacco advertising at sporting events by 2006.

While this may seem like a death knell for the industry, advertising bans in the past have actually strengthened the marketing position of the cigarette companies. That's because advertising bans tend to freeze market share and make it virtually impossible for a new competitor to enter the market. "Many observers have argued that previous interventions in the cigarette market suffered from the 'law of unintended consequences,' in the sense of having done more to protect the industry than promote the welfare of consumers," wrote the *Journal of Public Policy & Marketing* in 1996. "The 1971 broadcast advertising ban, which also ended free anti-smoking messages broadcast under the Federal Communication Commission's fairness doctrine, was probably counterproductive because its net effect was to reduce competition in the market but not to reduce smoking."[63]

5.

Dying to Smoke: Public Health

"For thy sake tobacco, I would do anything but die."
—CHARLES LAMB, *FAREWELL TO TOBACCO*

"If I cannot smoke in heaven, then I shall not go."
—MARK TWAIN

Hazardous to Your Health

In many ways, the basic mechanics of the cigarette business are similar to other industries. A company acquires raw materials, manufactures a good, and, aided by extensive marketing and advertising efforts, sells it to consumers. But there are two factors that make the business of selling cigarettes unique. The cigarette is addictive and therefore generates a captive audience that keeps coming back for more. And the cigarette is the only consumer product that, when used as the manufacturer has intended, can be deadly.

As a result, dealing with the health consequences of its products has become an unwelcome yet pervasive component of the cigarette business. Cigarette companies have invested mightily in research exploring the health effects of cigarettes, the nature of nicotine ad-

FIGURE 15:
Percentage of Deaths from Various Diseases Caused by Smoking in the Developed World

All causes	17%
All cancers	30%
Lung cancer	87%
Cancers of mouth and digestive tract	60%
Chronic lung disease	66%
Other respiratory diseases	10%
Heart disease	13%

SOURCE: World Health Organization.

diction, and ways to make cigarettes safer. As a result of those studies, the tobacco industry for much of the past 50 years has adopted a business strategy of cover-up and misinformation to suppress many of the more unseemly findings about the link between smoking and disease. At times, the industry has even used health worries to its advantage, creating new products like filters, low-tar cigarettes, and 100 percent "natural" cigarettes to assuage smokers' fears. More recently, when it became clear that acknowledging the health consequences of smoking could protect the industry from future liability, the tobacco companies have grudgingly admitted that smoking is a health risk. But what is most remarkable about the debate on smoking and health isn't so much the measures the government has taken to attack smoking, but the fact that the tobacco companies have been able to weather the storm at all.

What do we know about the harmful effects of smoking? The World Health Organization (WHO) estimates that tobacco kills 3.5 million people around the world annually, accounting for about 7 percent of all deaths worldwide. That number is expected to grow by 2020, when tobacco will be blamed for 17.7 percent of all deaths in the developed world and 10.9 percent of deaths in developing nations.[1]

Tobacco is the known or likely cause of about 25 diseases. It is said to be the most important cause of lung cancer, but also can cause cancer in the esophagus, mouth, throat, pancreas, kidney, and bladder. Smoking is a major risk factor for heart disease, stroke, and high blood pressure, and can cause pneumonia and chronic lung diseases. Maternal smoking is also associated with a higher risk of miscarriage, lower birth weight of babies, and inhibited child development. Smoking by parents is also a factor in sudden infant death syndrome and is associated with higher rates of respiratory illnesses among children.[2] [See Fig. 15]

On average, lifetime smokers have a 50 percent chance of dying from a tobacco-related illness, and half of those will die well before age 70, cutting an average of 22 years off their life expectancy. Smokers in their 30s and 40s are five times more likely to have a heart attack than nonsmokers.[3]

News that cigarettes are harmful isn't new. For nearly four centuries, physicians and scientists have suspected that smoking was bad for you. Even smoking skeptics outside the scientific community intuitively understood that drawing hot smelly smoke into the lungs didn't sound like a good idea. In 1602, one of the first known attacks on the smoking habit arrived in the form of a pamphlet called "Work for Chimney Sweeps." It noted that inhaled soot was the cause of disease among workers who cleaned chimneys and suggested that smokers faced similar peril.[4] It was in 1761—more than 200 years ago—that the first fears about a link between tobacco and cancer surfaced in a study that warned snuff users that they were vulnerable to cancers of the nose. Nearly 100 years later, in 1859, a French physician studied 68 patients with cancers of the nose and mouth and noted a link between the ailments and smoking. But he concluded that the problem stemmed from the heat of the clay pipes they smoked, not tobacco.[5]

Although tobacco use has long been linked to health problems, one of the most deadly diseases, lung cancer, was still extremely rare before the twentieth century. It's no coincidence that the rate of lung cancer began increasing with the popularity of the cigarette. Studies show that not only are cigarettes more addictive than other forms of tobacco, but that because the smoke is drawn deep into the lungs, they are significantly more harmful. Indeed, in 1919 a medical student named Alton Ochsner, who would later become a leading tobacco and health researcher, was summoned to witness an unusual autopsy. The dead man had died of lung cancer, and Dr. Ochsner's entire class was invited to witness the procedure because the chief surgeon was convinced the students were not likely to see another case of lung cancer during their careers.[6]

But it wasn't until the 1930s, a time when cigarette smoking had surged in popularity, that a growing body of scientific research began suggesting the toxic nature of cigarettes. In 1933, *Scientific American* reported that a Chicago researcher had tentatively linked the "tar" in cigarette smoke to a recent increase in lung cancer cases.[7] Tobacco company records show that in 1946, a Lorillard scientist noted that cigarettes "possess definite carcinogenic properties."[8]

But it was a *Reader's Digest* article in 1952 entitled "Cancer by the Carton" that prompted widespread worry about the links between smoking and cancer. The article, which summarized the scientific research on the subject, represented the first time the mainstream press had suggested that the true danger of smoking had been hidden from the public. Those fears were compounded in 1953, when the journal *Cancer Research* published an alarming study by Dr. Ernest Wynder. Dr. Wynder had painted smoke condensate on the skin of mice, and 44 percent of the animals developed cancerous tumors. In December of that year, a British health minister noted that, despite a lack of conclusive scientific data, the statistical evidence "does point to a causal relationship between tobacco smoking and lung cancer."[9]

The cancer talk began taking a toll on cigarette sales, which fell from a peak of 416 billion packs in 1952 to 384 billion in 1953.[10] This fact, of course, didn't go unnoticed by the nation's tobacco executives, who on December 15, 1953, gathered together at an unusual meeting in Manhattan's Plaza hotel. The gathering was risky because the last time a similar group had gotten together was in 1939, and they had subsequently been prosecuted for price fixing.

According to a memo of the meeting, the chief executives of all the major tobacco companies of the day—American Tobacco, R. J. Reynolds, Benson & Hedges, B.S. Tobacco Co., and Brown & Williamson—attended. Liggett & Myers wasn't there because the "company feels that the proper procedure is to ignore the whole controversy," according to the memo of the meeting. Also in attendance was John Hill of Hill & Knowlton, a growing public relations firm that had been called in to help the tobacco companies deal with the crisis.

The group decided a public relations campaign was the best way to deal with what was now often referred to as "the heath question." American Tobacco Co. president Paul Hahn suggested the group form an informal committee named the "Tobacco Industry Committee for Public Information." Hill, the public relations guru, suggested the world "research" be added to the title, and the group agreed on the "Tobacco Industry Research Committee" (TIRC).[11]

The Hill & Knowlton memo goes on to describe the executives' resolve to counter the growing fears and body of scientific evidence that indicated their products were dangerous. The group agreed that the health pressures facing their industry were "extremely serious and worthy of drastic action."

The industry is strongly convinced that there is no sound scientific basis for the charges that have been made. They believe that the more sensational accusations in the recent papers were

premature and in some cases represent publicity issued in the
hopes of attracting funds and support for further research.

They point out that the National Cancer Institute of the
U.S. Public Health Administration, which is a government
agency and supported by Congressional appropriations, has of-
ficially refuted the tie-up between cigarette smoking and can-
cer. Nevertheless, they realize the industry should not engage
merely in a defensive campaign, replying to and answering in-
dividual research papers or magazine articles. They feel that
they should sponsor a public relations campaign which is pos-
itive in nature and is entirely "pro-cigarettes." They are confi-
dent they can supply us with comprehensive and authoritative
scientific material which completely refutes the health
charges.[12]

The assertion that the committee could scientifically debunk
the health concerns was made at a time when many of the companies had already compiled their own evidence of the risks of
smoking. Earlier that same year, a Reynolds researcher wrote that
"studies of clinical data tend to confirm the relationship between
heavy and prolonged tobacco smoking and incidence of cancer of
the lung."[13]

Hill, as outlined in the memo, continued to question the
executives about their commitment to uncovering the truth about
cigarettes and health. The executives "wholeheartedly agreed to the
principle," that "public health is paramount to all else." But they
balked at Hill's suggestion that they sponsor additional health
research.

A clear-cut answer to this question was deferred for the time
being. The companies all say that they are carrying on much
more research in their own laboratories and are sponsoring
more research at hospitals and universities than is generally rec-
ognized. They believe that when we are acquainted with all of

*the scientific and factual material in the hands of the compa-
nies, we will agree that the major problem is to disseminate
information on hand rather than to conduct new research.
However, John Hill did not agree to this and emphatically
warned the companies that they should probably expect to
sponsor additional research.*[14]

Even in the earliest days of panic about the dangers of cigarette smoking, the nation's tobacco executives were prescient in
predicting that the health scare was not a temporary blip on the
radar screens of cigarette makers.

*They are also emphatic in saying that the entire activity is a
long-term, continuing program, since they feel that the problem
is one of promoting cigarettes and protecting them from these
and other attacks that may be expected in the future. Each of
the company presidents attending emphasized the fact that they
consider the program to be a long-term one.*[15]

The TIRC quickly got to work, and on January 5, 1954,
issued "A Frank Statement to Cigarette Smokers," which it placed
in 448 newspapers in the United States. It stated:

*Recent reports on experiments with mice have given wide
publicity to a theory that cigarette smoking is in some way
linked with lung cancer in human beings.*

*Although conducted by doctors of professional standing,
these experiments are not regarded as conclusive in the field of
cancer research. However, we do not believe the results are
inconclusive, should be disregarded or lightly dismissed. At the
same time, we feel it is in the public interest to call attention to
the fact that eminent doctors and research scientists have publicly questioned the claimed significance of these experiments.*

Distinguished authorities point out:

That medical research of recent years indicates many possible causes of lung cancer.

That there is no agreement among the authorities regarding what the cause is.

That there is no proof that cigarette smoking is one of the causes.

That statistics purporting to link cigarette smoking with the disease could apply with equal force to any one of many other aspects of modern life. Indeed, the validity of the statistics themselves is questioned by numerous scientists.

We accept an interest in people's health as a basic responsibility, paramount to every other consideration in our business.

We believe the products we make are not injurious to health.

We always have and always will cooperate closely with those whose task it is to safeguard the public health.

For more than 300 years, tobacco has given solace, relaxation and enjoyment to mankind. At one time or another during those years, critics have held it responsible for practically every disease of the human body. One by one these charges have been abandoned for lack of evidence.

Regardless of the record of the past, the fact that cigarette smoking today should even be suspected as a cause of a serious disease is a matter of deep concern to us.

Many people have asked us what we are doing to meet the public's concerns roused by the recent reports. Here is the answer:

We are pledging aid and assistance to the research effort into all phases of tobacco use and health. This joint financial aid will of course be in addition to what is already being contributed by individual companies. For this purpose we are establishing a joint industry group consisting initially of the undersigned. This group will be known as the Tobacco Industry Research Committee.

In charge of the research activities of the committee will be

a scientist of unimpeachable integrity and national repute. In
addition there will be an advisory board of scientists disinter-
ested in the cigarette industry. A group of distinguished men
from medicine, science and education will be invited to serve
on this board. These scientists will advise the committee on its
research activities.

This statement is being issued because we believe the people
are entitled to know where we stand on this matter and what
we intend to do about it.[16]

True to its word, the committee did hire an eminent scientist,
Dr. Clarence Cook Little, the former head of the National Cancer
Institute, which later was renamed the American Cancer Society.
But even though Dr. Little's credentials were impeccable, he came
to the job with a bias that favored the tobacco companies' position. Dr. Little had spent his career focusing on the genetic origins
of cancer, and he was already convinced that environmental factors, such as smoking, didn't play a role in the disease.[17]

The TIRC also that year released "A Scientific Perspective on
the Cigarette Controversy," a booklet quoting 36 scientists who
questioned the link between smoking and disease. The report was
carried in hundreds of newspapers and on radio stations around
the United States, and was also widely distributed to 177,000 doctors and other medical professionals.[18]

In the years following the formation of the Tobacco Industry
Research Committee, the industry continued to downplay the
health worries. A new study involving mice with the tar-induced
tumors, for instance, wasn't relevant, the TIRC asserted, because
animal experiments couldn't be applied to humans. The tobacco
companies also began offering new products that it promised
would reduce the risk of health problems. Brown & Williamson
began promoting its Viceroy cigarettes with a "health-guard" filter,
and in ads claimed the brand was "better for your health than any
other leading cigarette." Philip Morris touted "the cigarette that

takes the FEAR out of smoking," and Lorillard advertised that its Kent brand "takes out more nicotine and tars than any other leading cigarette—the difference in protection is priceless." L&M even ran ads featuring Barbara Stanwyck and Rosalind Russell touting L&M's new "miracle product," a filter that is "just what the doctor ordered."[19]

But this part of the strategy backfired. The advent of "fear" advertising was widely blamed by industry executives for increasing, rather than abating, worries about cigarettes and health. And the fear ads, along with continuing scientific research implicating cigarettes, are believed to have contributed to a continued decline in cigarette sales. In 1955, the Federal Trade Commission banned advertising claims about "the presence or absence of any health effect of smoking." Ironically, the government mandate inadvertently helped boost cigarette sales. Following the cessation of the fear ads in 1955, cigarette sales rebounded for the rest of the decade.[20]

Although the tobacco companies were taking a public stance that there was no link between smoking and cancer, the companies' own researchers were discovering otherwise. In 1956, an RJR chemist authored a paper called "The Analysis of Cigarette Smoking Condensate." One of his findings: "Since it is now well established that cigarette smoke does contain several polycyclic aromatic hydrocarbons, and considering the potential and actual carcinogenic activity of a number of these compounds, a method of either complete removal or almost complete removal of these compounds from smoke is required."[21] And by 1957, BAT was using a code word for cancer—Zephyr. "As a result of several statistical surveys, the idea has arisen that there is a causal relationship between Zephyr and tobacco smoking, particularly cigarette smoking," states one memo.[22]

That same year, both British and U.S. health authorities announced that there was increasing evidence of a causal relationship between smoking and cancer.[23] The industry continued to deny the link, and in 1958 formed the Tobacco Institute to take over the industry's public relations efforts. Even so, executives within the industry were beginning to have their own doubts about the "health question." "All of us, or at least most of us, in the tobacco industry are caught between a guilt complex and a power complex," states a confidential Philip Morris memo in April 1958. "The guilt complex is a simple matter. We tend to suffer from the sternly repressed fear that our opponents are right and we are wrong on the health question and that we are thus devoting our business lives to the propagation of lung cancer."[24]

As a result of the many conflicting health claims and the industry-propagated fear ads, an air of uncertainty remained around the smoking and health issue. A Gallup survey in 1958 found that only 44 percent of respondents believed smoking caused cancer.[25]

But a Saturday morning in 1964 proved to be a significant turning point in the scientific debate about smoking. On that day, Surgeon General Luther L. Terry distributed a 387-page report entitled "Smoking and Health: Report of the Advisory Committee to the Surgeon General of the Public Health Service." Terry had convened a panel of some of the country's most respected scientists, selecting only those who hadn't taken a stand on the smoking issue. The finding was cautious, yet still dramatic. "It is the judgment of the committee that cigarette smoking contributes substantially to mortality from certain specific diseases and to the overall death rate."[26]

They found a causal link between smoking and lung cancer in men, and noted that the data for women, though sparse, "point in the same direction." It noted that the death rate for smokers was 70 percent higher than nonsmokers, and that men who smoked were ten times as likely to die of lung cancer. The report concluded: "Cigarette smoking is a health hazard of sufficient importance in the United States to warrant appropriate remedial action."[27]

The report carried a surprising amount of weight with the

American public as well as with politicians, who began pushing for warning labels on cigarettes. Surprisingly, the American Medical Association (AMA) sided with the tobacco industry, opposing the labels. The AMA, incidentally, had earlier the same year accepted a $10 million grant for tobacco research from six tobacco companies.[28] Nonetheless, the labeling regulations were approved, and by 1966, the health warning "Caution: Cigarette Smoking May Be Hazardous to Your Health" was required on all cigarette packs. By 1968, polls showed that 78 percent of Americans now believed smoking caused cancer, while per capita consumption of cigarettes fell from 210 packs in 1967 to about 200 in 1969.[29] By 1970, the percentage of smokers among the adult population in the United States had dropped to 37 percent, down from about 50 percent in the 1950s.[30]

The 1970s marked a continuation of the assault on the industry. In early 1970, the *New York Times* reported on a now-famous "smoking beagles" study by scientist Oscar Auerbach, in which 12 out of 86 dogs taught to smoke had developed lung cancer. It was the first time cancer had been produced in large animals exposed to tobacco smoke.[31] The study rattled tobacco industry researchers. A researcher at the British tobacco company Gallaher Ltd. said in a memo: "We are of the opinion that the Auerbach work proves beyond reasonable doubt the causation of lung cancer by smoke."[32] Two months after the smoking beagles study, RJR abruptly shut down one of its own research facilities dubbed the "Mouse House" because of work researchers there had conducted with smoking rats and emphysema.[33] It would be the first of several industry labs that were closed over the next several years as the tobacco companies, alarmed by what their own researchers were learning about cigarettes, ended internal research efforts as a way to guard against future liability.

In 1971, the Royal College of Physicians in Great Britain published a controversial report comparing the cigarette epidemic to a "holocaust." The report found that cigarette smoking was as

Smoking-Related Deaths in the United States

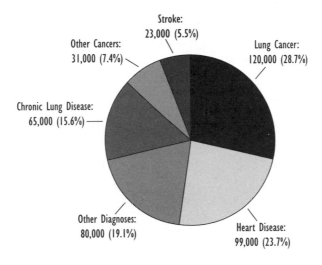

Stroke:
23,000 (5.5%)

Other Cancers:
31,000 (7.4%)

Lung Cancer:
120,000 (28.7%)

Chronic Lung Disease:
65,000 (15.6%)

Other Diagnoses:
80,000 (19.1%)

Heart Disease:
99,000 (23.7%)

SOURCE: Centers for Disease Control.

important a cause of death as the great epidemic diseases such as typhoid, cholera, and tuberculosis that had afflicted previous generations.[34] Not long after the report, the British government ordered health warnings on cigarettes to read: "Warning by HM Government: Smoking Can Damage Your Health." In the United States, warning labels were strengthened to read, "Warning: The Surgeon General Has Determined That Cigarette Smoking Is Dangerous to Your Health." [See Fig. 16] The health crusade against cigarettes was gaining momentum. Tobacco ads were taken off the air, and health warnings were added to other cigarette advertisements. Nonetheless, the industry's strategy of denial throughout this onslaught of negative press seemed to be working. Smoking rates continued to slide, but not as dramatically as in earlier decades. By the end of the 1970s, 33.5 percent of the population still smoked.[35]

In the 1980s, despite irrefutable evidence from government health researchers and internal industry research linking smoking and disease, the tobacco companies continued to refute the health concerns. In 1981, BAT's director of research and development told the *Confectionary and Tobacco News*: "Despite a never-ending stream of research on the possible health hazards of smoking, there is no proof of a cause and effect relationship between cigarette smoking and various alleged smoking diseases."[36] And in a briefing to industry analysts, RJR's chairman stated: "We believe that the campaign against tobacco is based on statistical inferences unsupported by clinical findings."[37] Several industry executives also tried a new tactic, stating that they weren't medical doctors and simply couldn't comment on any medical or health issues associated with their product.[38]

But in the 1980s, the tobacco industry faced a venerable opponent in the form of U.S. Surgeon General C. Everett Koop. With his sideburns, graying beard, and white military uniform, Koop looked like he'd arrived straight from central casting. And unlike his predecessors, Koop didn't mince words when it came to tobacco. He started a public relations campaign calling for a "smokeless society by the year 2000," and branded the industry "sleazy" and accused them of "flat-footed lies" when they claimed there was no proof that smoking caused cancer.[39] In 1982 he issued his first report on smoking saying that "cigarette smoking . . . is the chief single avoidable cause of death in our society and the most important public health issue of our time."[40]

A memo in February 1982 from Philip Morris researcher J. L. Charles summed up the industry reaction to Koop's crusade against smoking.

> *This company is in trouble. The cigarette industry is in trouble. If we are to survive as a viable commercial enterprise, we must act now to develop responses to smoking and health allegations from both the private and the government sectors. The anti-smoking forces are out to bury us. . . .*

Let's face facts: Cigarette smoke is biologically active.
Nicotine is a potent pharmacological agent. Every toxicologist,
physiologist, medical doctor and most chemists know that. It's
not a secret.[41]

Koop continued his attack on the industry with several additional reports linking smoking to cardiovascular and lung diseases and crusaded against "secondhand smoke" in his 1986 report, "The Health Consequences of Involuntary Smoking." He attacked nicotine and spoke with such conviction about the harmful effects of smoking that his presence in the Surgeon General's office changed the tenor of the smoking debate. All of a sudden, it was simply common knowledge that smoking caused cancers, and the industry's continual denials now sounded implausible.

In a bid to save their credibility, the cigarette makers by the 1990s began to acknowledge that smoking carried some "risk," as Philip Morris stated in its 1991 annual report.

We have acknowledged that smoking is a risk factor in the
development of lung cancer and certain diseases because a statis-
tical relationship exists between smoking and the occurrence of
these diseases. Accordingly we insist that the decision to smoke,
like many other lifestyle decisions, should be made by informed
adults. We believe that smokers around the world are well aware
of the potential risks associated with tobacco use, and have the
knowledge necessary to make an informed decision.[42]

By the early 1990s, about 80 countries required health warnings on tobacco packages.[43] The United Kingdom in 1992 didn't mince words with its new health warnings that read: "Smoking Kills." But the World Health Organization complained that in most countries, the warnings remained inconspicuous and didn't provide enough information about the serious consequences of tobacco use.[44]

Although the industry's strategy for dealing with the health effects of its products for years has centered on denial, that stance has recently changed dramatically. In 1998—more than 50 years after tobacco industry researchers found a link between smoking and cancer—Liggett Group publicly admitted that cigarettes are addictive and harmful to smokers' health. The admission wasn't done out of altruism, but out of a shrewd calculation of the business consequences of denial. Liggett Group, the smallest of the big U.S. tobacco companies, used the concession to end a legal assault on the company by cooperating with the government and plaintiffs' attorneys.[45] More recently, Brown & Williamson, billing itself as a "responsible company in a controversial industry," has created a web site that warns smokers about the risk of using the company's products, even referring them to organizations that could help them quit. A B&W spokesman says the site is simply to give smokers information, although industry analysts note that the dissemination of health warnings by B&W via the Internet likely will shield the company from future legal attacks by the current generation of smokers.[46]

The history of the cigarette industry's strategy for dealing with the harmful effects of smoking counters the image of Big Tobacco simply careening from crisis to crisis in the debate about smoking and health. For years the cigarette industry has been aware of the mounting health worries about its products. Managing the problem, through public relations, advertising, and the funding of scientific research aimed at refuting the claims, has been a core part of the industry's business strategy for nearly five decades. "Public relations forestalled any serious look at the issue or any conscience-searching at the time," writes Philip J. Hilts in *Smokescreen: The Truth Behind the Tobacco Industry Cover-up*. "There is no case like it in the annals of business or health."[47]

The "Safe" Cigarette

Although the cigarette industry has spent much of the past fifty years denying a link between smoking and disease, the industry has also dedicated a significant amount of time and money to develop a "safe" cigarette. A safe cigarette that can both satisfy smokers' demands for taste and nicotine delivery and placate public health concerns is the Holy Grail of the tobacco industry. The company that comes up with it first likely could dominate the entire industry by selling the newfangled smoke at a significant premium and grabbing market share from its competitors. Indeed, in the 1950s, Philip Morris researchers already saw the potential of a "healthy" cigarette and had even begun to suggest that the company could capitalize on health concerns by admitting that cigarettes were harmful. "Evidence is building up that heavy smoking contributes to lung cancer," wrote a Philip Morris scientist in July 1958. He then suggested that the company have the "intestinal fortitude to jump to the other side of the fence," and that the company would have a "wealth of ammunition" to attack competitors who did not have safer cigarettes.[48]

But several factors have stood in the way of the development of a safer smoke. Taking the toxins out of cigarette smoke has turned out to be a technological challenge. The biggest problem has been maintaining the taste and smoking sensations that smokers crave—so far, no company has overcome those obstacles. And industry lawyers have balked at the suggestions that cigarette makers embark on research to make safe cigarettes out of fears of the tricky legal problem such research would create for the entire industry. Patrick Sheehy, the former chief executive of British American Tobacco, wrote in 1986 that safe cigarette research would be a tacit admission that cigarettes are dangerous. "In attempting to develop a 'safe' cigarette you are, by implication, in danger of being interpreted as accepting the current product is unsafe and this is not a position that I think we should take," he wrote.[49]

Finally, the safe cigarette has been stymied by the very groups who are most concerned about the health effects of smoking: antitobacco groups and public health officials. The cigarette industry's efforts to market safer cigarettes have been met with fierce opposition by antitobacco activists, who want to see such products labeled as nicotine delivery devices and subjected to government regulations. Although the opposition of health groups to a safe cigarette would seem contradictory, it is borne out of a deep mistrust of the cigarette companies, whose strategy of denial over the years has created a credibility gap with the public health community.

The cigarette makers first began making noises about safer cigarettes in the 1950s during a period now known among historians as the "tar derby." As a result of growing public concerns about smoking and health, the cigarette makers responded with a variety of new filter cigarettes that would ostensibly reduce tar levels. But the rise of the filter cigarette was more a marketing ploy than anything else. There was little evidence to suggest that filter cigarettes were any healthier than regular cigarettes, and the tobacco companies, own researchers knew this to be the case. A 1976 memo from Ernest Pepples, Brown & Williamson's vice president and general counsel, noted that filter cigarettes surged from less than 1 percent of the market in 1950 to 87 percent in 1975. "In most cases, however, the smoker of a filter cigarette was getting as much or more nicotine and tar as he would have gotten from a regular cigarette. He had abandoned the regular cigarette, however, on the ground of reduced risk to health," wrote Pepples.[50]

Even today, many smokers think that low-tar or so-called light or ultra-light cigarettes are better for them than full-strength smokes. Because reducing tar levels also tends to lower nicotine levels, studies have shown that smokers inadvertently compensate for the loss of the nicotine. Smokers of low-tar cigarettes inhale more deeply, take puffs more often, and even cover up the tiny holes near the filter that were put there to reduce the amount of smoke, and subsequently the amount of tar, that a smoker inhales.

During the 1960s cigarette makers embarked on extensive research to create a safe cigarette. The goal was to remove the toxins from a conventional cigarette without altering the taste or smoking experience. Memos from that time period show that some tobacco company executives were genuinely interested not only in profits but in making their products healthier. In 1962, Charles Ellis, a British American Tobacco research executive, noted that painting mice with "fresh" smoke condensate, more similar to the "fresh" smoke inhaled by smokers, might prove to be more harmful than the older, stored condensate often used in such experiments. "This possibility need not dismay us, indeed it would mean that there really was a chemical culprit somewhere in smoke, and one, moreover, that underwent a reaction fairly quickly to something else. I feel confident that in this case we could identify this group of substances, and it would be worth almost any effort, by preliminary treatment, additives or filtration, to get rid of it."[51]

Industry documents show that tobacco companies focused their safe-cigarette research on several areas, including the development of synthetic tobacco, boosting nicotine levels in low-tar cigarettes (so smokers wouldn't have to compensate for a loss of nicotine), and selective filtration of the most toxic substances in cigarette smoke, such as carbon monoxide.[52] Research into safe cigarettes also has focused on the removal or lowering of four types of carcinogenic compounds: nitrosamines, widely viewed as the most deadly cancer-causing agents in tobacco smoke; aldehydes, formed by the burning of sugars and cellulose in tobacco; polycyclic aromatic hydrocarbons, which form in the cigarette behind the burning tip; and traces of heavy metals present in tobacco as a result of fertilizers used on the plant.[53]

But despite the industry's early optimism about simply removing the toxic elements from a cigarette, the quest for a safe cigarette proved to be a technically and politically daunting challenge. Industry researchers often found ways of lowering one or two of the dangerous compounds, only to discover that their tinkering had either increased the level of some other harmful compound or so dramatically altered the cigarette that it wouldn't be accepted by consumers. In 1975, Brown & Williamson introduced a new cigarette, Fact, which had been designed to selectively remove certain compounds, including cyanide, from cigarette smoke. But the product was pulled from the market after just two years. Scientists also experimented with tobacco substitutes, including ingredients made with wood pulp, that were said to be less toxic than tobacco. But those products ran into a new set of problems because they were no longer a naturally occurring tobacco product but a synthetic creation about which health claims were being made. That meant government regulators viewed the tobacco substitutes more like drugs, subjecting them to a regulatory morass that the cigarette makers wanted to avoid. In 1977, a few British tobacco companies, Imperial, Gallaher, and Rothmans, which could avoid U.S. Food and Drug Administration scrutiny, launched several versions of cigarettes made with tobacco substitutes. But the products met with resistance from health groups, who claimed the new cigarettes were still unsafe, and the products floundered and were withdrawn after just a few months.

In the 1970s, Liggett Group Inc. embarked on its own safe-cigarette program known as the "XA Project." The project focused on blending additives to tobacco to neutralize cancer-causing compounds. The company discovered that blending certain catalysts with tobacco would destroy polycyclic aromatic hydrocarbons— the dangerous compounds which form behind the cigarette's burning tip. The problem was, the company had demonstrated this in mouse skin painting tests—the same type of test conducted by Ernest Wynder that the entire tobacco industry had spent years debunking. Nonetheless, skin painting tests related to the XA Project showed that cancerous tumors were virtually eliminated when the catalyst was added to tobacco.

Liggett faced a marketing problem if it pursued the XA Project cigarettes. How could the company market the benefits of the XA Project cigarettes without making health claims that would subject it to government scrutiny? And how could the company promote mouse skin tests as proof their new cigarettes worked at the same time its lawyers were in courtrooms challenging the validity of mouse tests while defending the company against smokers' lawsuits? A former industry lawyer now says that Liggett was pressured by other cigarette makers to abandon the effort because the "marketing and sale of a safe cigarette could result in infinite liability in civil litigation as it would constitute a direct or implied admission that all other cigarettes were unsafe."[54] Liggett eventually abandoned the project.

By the early 1980s, other cigarette makers also had abandoned many of their efforts to develop a safe cigarette. In addition to the technological hurdles they faced, industry lawyers had grown increasingly wary about the research, and the concession, implicit in such research, that existing cigarettes weren't safe. Nonetheless, more than 150 patents related to designing safe cigarettes have been filed in the United States and the United Kingdom during the past 25 years.[55] Tobacco executives say the fact that a patent has been filed doesn't mean the product is necessarily marketable or acceptable to consumers, but the sheer volume of patents shows that the industry has invested heavily in developing a safer cigarette even as its own executives were denying any link between smoking and disease. And there are now several claims from former industry workers that many tobacco companies shelved research into safer products out of fear of exposing themselves to additional liability. In 1998, for instance, a former Philip Morris researcher testified that the company shelved promising research to remove cadmium, a lung irritant, from tobacco plants.[56]

Despite such criticism, the major cigarette makers have attempted to market several versions of safer cigarettes. In 1988, RJR introduced a high-tech cigarette called Premier. Premier, touted as a virtually smokeless cigarette that dramatically reduced the cancer-causing compounds inhaled by smokers, was made of aluminum capsules that contained tobacco pellets. The pellets were heated instead of burned, thereby producing less smoke and ash than traditional cigarettes. Although the product looked like a traditional cigarette, it required its own instruction booklet showing consumers how to light it.

From the beginning, Premier had several strikes against it. RJR had spent an estimated $800 million developing the brand, and the total cost was expected to soar to $1 billion by the time it was placed in national distribution. The costly project was put into test market just as Kohlberg Kravis Roberts & Co. had embarked on a $25 billion leveraged buyout of RJR that had saddled the company with debt. And the cigarette faced a lengthy regulatory battle after public health officials argued it should be regulated by the FDA as a drug. But the biggest problem with Premier was the fact that consumers simply couldn't get used to it. Many smokers complained about the taste, which some smokers said left a charcoal taste in their mouths. RJR had also gambled that smokers would be willing to give Premier several tries before making a final decision about whether to smoke it. RJR estimated that to acquire a taste for Premier, smokers would have to consume two or three packs to be won over. But as it turned out, most smokers took one cigarette and shared the rest of the pack with friends, and few bothered to buy it again. RJR scrapped the brand in early 1989, less than a year after it was introduced.[57]

In 1989, Philip Morris entered the fray with a virtually nicotine-free cigarette called Next that it claimed was better than other low-nicotine varieties because its taste was indistinguishable from regular cigarettes. The nicotine was removed from Next using high-pressure carbon dioxide in a process similar to the method used by coffee companies when making decaffeinated coffee. It was even marketed similarly to decaffeinated coffee. Next cigarettes were touted for their "rich flavor" and referred to as "de-nic" cigarettes. But tobacco critics complained that Next actually had higher tar levels than many cigarettes, and that heavy smokers would simply smoke more Next cigarettes to give their bodies the nicotine they crave. The product flopped and was withdrawn.[58]

Despite those setbacks, both RJR and Philip Morris have tried again with high-tech versions of smokeless cigarettes. In 1994, RJR began testing the Eclipse smokeless cigarette, which claimed to reduce secondhand smoke by 85 to 90 percent. Eclipse is more like an ordinary cigarette than its predecessor Premier because it contains tobacco and reconstituted tobacco. But it also includes a charcoal tip that, when lighted, heats glycerin added to the cigarette but doesn't burn the tobacco. The result is a cigarette that emits tobacco flavor without creating the ash and smoke. But RJR isn't touting Eclipse as a safe cigarette, instead marketing it as a more socially acceptable product less offensive to nonsmokers. Indeed, because Eclipse still burns some tobacco, it has tar levels similar to those of ultra-light cigarettes already on the market. Eclipse emits lower tar levels of cancer-causing compounds than many existing cigarettes, but it still produces carbon monoxide and nicotine. And questions have also been raised about the effects of heating glycerin. When burned, glycerin is known to be carcinogenic. It also remains unclear whether the FDA will attempt to regulate Eclipse if RJR launches it nationally.[59]

Philip Morris is testing its own high-tech cigarette called Accord, which has been described as a cigarette encased in a Kazoo-shaped lighter. Consumers buy a $40 kit that includes a battery charger, a puff-activated lighter that holds the cigarette, and a carton of special cigarettes. To smoke the cigarettes, a smoker sucks on the kazoolike box. A microchip senses the puff and sends a burst of heat to the cigarette. The process gives the smoker one drag and doesn't create ashes or smoke. An illuminated display shows the number of puffs remaining, and the batteries must be recharged after every pack. It's unclear whether smokers will find the low-smoke and -ash benefits desirable enough to justify learning an entirely new smoking ritual. Although Philip Morris doesn't make health claims about Accord, the company in 1998 told the Society of Toxicology that Accord generated 83 percent fewer toxins than a regular cigarette.[60]

Perhaps the most promising new technology to make a safer cigarette lies in research to lower nitrosamines, those prevalent and deadly cancer-causing compounds in cigarettes. Brown & Williamson and RJR are developing cigarettes that use a special tobacco with lower nitrosamine content. The tobacco is cured with a special process that inhibits the formation of nitrosamines. But Brown & Williamson isn't planning to tout the health benefits of the nitrosamine-free smoke. "We can't be sure nitrosamine-free tobacco is necessarily safer," a B&W spokeswoman told the *Wall Street Journal.* "We don't want to claim the product is safer unless we are sure it is. It's a bit of a muggy area."[61]

Although public health officials describe the quest for a nitrosamine-free cigarette as a step in the right direction, the research still raises concerns that smokers could be lulled into a false sense of security. Cigarettes without nitrosamines still produce other carcinogens, scientists say, and more smokers die of heart-related ailments than cancer. As Dietrich Hoffmann of the American Health Foundation says, "The best cigarette is no cigarette."

The Last Cigarette

One of the most remarkable aspects of the cigarette business is the fact that today, most smokers and nonsmokers—at least those who live in the developed world—know that cigarette smoking can cause disease or even death. Each cigarette is said to take seven minutes off the life of a smoker, and the majority of smokers say they want to quit.[62] Nonetheless, the cigarette industry continues to exist—even thrive—under some of the most adverse business conditions faced by any modern industry.

Do the tobacco companies shoulder all the blame for the cigarette "epidemic"? To be sure, the cigarette makers have spent the past 50 years denying overwhelming evidence that smoking caus-es cancer and other disease. And the industry has fueled interest in its product with slick advertising and product promotions. But since the earliest days of the discovery of tobacco, long before any of the cigarette makers came on to the scene, men and women have been drawn to the habit. Charles Lemaistre, past president of the American Cancer Society, called it "one of the most grievous examples of destructive behavior in the history of mankind."[63]

Why do people start smoking? The reasons people are attract-ed to this strange ritual are complex and at the very core of human nature. For most people, the first smoking experience is an unpleasant one, accompanied by nausea, light-headedness, cough-ing, and gagging—hardly an endorsement for a second cigarette. Yet many of them continue to smoke.

Clearly the image of cigarette smoking plays a role. During to-bacco's earliest days, it was quickly labeled a vice and as a result car-ried with it the allure of the forbidden. Even before modern cigarette makers weighed in, tobacco was viewed as an adult pas-time, giving it an inherent appeal among children. Today, hip im-ages of smoking actors and actresses and sexy ads showing the cigarette's glamorous side all contribute to the reasons young peo-ple start smoking. Studies have shown that the controversy sur-rounding smoking, particularly in the United States and developed nations, has enhanced the appeal of cigarettes among potential smokers. Several sociologists and psychologists have studied the science of consumer warning labels and discovered that many warnings backfire, often enticing people into the very behavior they are trying to prevent. One State University of New York study noted that when "No Diving" signs were posted around swimming pools, for instance, teenage boys looked at the signs and dove in. And in Europe, which has some of the most dire cigarette warnings such as "Smoking Kills" and "Smokers Die Younger," smoking rates are significantly higher than other countries with less strin-gent appeals.[64]

As a result of this phenomenon, researchers have long studied the "personality" of smoking, and discovered that the habit appeals to a particular type of person. So who smokes? You are more likely to be a smoker if you are poor or poorly educated. Smokers are more likely to be divorced and less likely to wear seat belts. Smokers are more likely to be high-risk takers and sensation seekers. Smokers are more likely to feel that their lives are subject to chance, that they have little control over the things that happen to them. They are more likely to be rebellious and defiant. Smokers have a higher sex drive than nonsmokers and tend to be impulsive. Many smokers have a history of depression.[65]

Psychologist Ernest Dichter in 1948 conducted an extensive study on the reasons people smoke. Today, some of his conclusions seem a bit naive, given that he didn't address the issue of whether smoking was addictive or harmful. But he did recognize many of the social and emotional reasons smokers smoke. In "Why Do We Smoke Cigarettes?" Dichter recognized the importance of the smoking ritual and noted that the cigarette was often used to both measure and pass the time. (He called the cigarette "a modern hourglass.") He believed people smoked because it was fun, because it provided a simple reward and offered companionship—the cigarette was a friend during times of solitude and served as a conversation starter that helped bring people together. He noted that smokers simply enjoy watching the smoke that cigarettes create, and he believed that cigarettes appealed to man's primal fascination with fire. He also noted that smokers believed cigarettes made them more mentally alert and also helped them to relax. He concluded:

> *If we consider all the pleasure and advantages provided, in a most democratic and international fashion, by this little white paper roll, we shall understand why it is difficult to destroy its power by means of warnings, threats, or preachings. This pleasure miracle has so much to offer that we can safely*

predict the cigarette is here to stay. Our psychological analysis
is not intended as a eulogy of the habit of smoking, but rather
as an objective report on why people smoke cigarettes. Perhaps
this will seem more convincing if we reveal a personal secret:
We ourselves do not smoke at all. We may be missing a great
deal.[66]

Although Dichter ignored the addictive nature of cigarettes, he recognized that many smokers genuinely believe that they benefit in many ways from the habit. And science has shown that smokers do reap certain rewards from cigarettes well beyond mere taste enjoyment or the pleasure of the smoking ritual. David Krogh devotes an entire book, *Smoking: The Artificial Passion*, to his quest to discover the reasons people smoke. He asks, "Can nicotine produce absolute enhancements in human performance?" Several studies show that it can.

In one test, subjects were asked to watch the second hand of a clock. Occasionally, the hand would pause for just three-hundredths of a second, and those taking the test were asked to push a button at that moment. After a matter of minutes, the test, as you might expect, grows tedious, and the subjects' reaction time slows and some miss the pauses altogether. But interestingly, smokers who were allowed to smoke during the 80-minute test performed far better than nonsmokers or smokers who were forced to abstain from smoking.

In another test, nonsmokers were given nicotine doses and then asked to tap rapidly on a computer keyboard. The subjects could tap about 5 percent faster on nicotine than without it.

Dozens of other experiments support the view that smoking can enhance performance. Broadly, these tests show that nicotine can help people maintain their concentration over time and helps them "filter" out distractions. This would explain, in part, why smoking tends to be a "working drug"—a drug that, unlike heroin or alcohol, can be consumed in the workplace without impairing, and even perhaps enhancing, performance. "Smoking is not just a matter of being shackled to an addiction," notes Krogh. "It's an aid, a kind of trick if you wish, to help people function."[67]

Krogh sees other benefits of smoking as well. Smoking clearly has a calming effect on its user. In experiments that measure fatigue and aggression, smokers often fare better than nonsmokers. One test asked subjects to play a kind of electronic game in which they hit buttons that would either allow them to accumulate money, take money away from their competitor, or blast their competitor with white noise. Blasting with noise and taking money away from a competitor were viewed as aggressive tactics. The results of the study showed that the smokers, their bodies suffused with nicotine, were less aggressive than those playing without the aid of nicotine. "Nicotine moderates mood shifts that are brought about by stressful influences," writes Krogh. "It seems to diminish aggression, while helping people to maintain sociability and an even tone. Just as important, it does these things without having a generalized numbing effect."[68]

Another benefit, notable given the smoking rates among women, is the fact that smoking helps people stay thinner. When a regular smoker quits, he or she typically gains an average of six pounds. And smokers, on average, weigh about seven pounds less than nonsmokers. (Krogh notes that some studies show smokers weigh an average of 15 pounds less than comparable groups of nonsmokers.) Possible reasons for the lower weights of smokers include the fact that nicotine dulls the craving for sweet foods, and smokers often snack less because they smoke. Nicotine has also been shown to promote slight increases in metabolism.[69]

"If we ask why [smoking] has been so wildly popular with the human race, we can now offer a partial answer," Krogh says. "Because it does a lot of different things for different people."[70]

Krogh and other researchers acknowledge that the primary reason smokers smoke is to get nicotine into their bodies. As noted tobacco researcher M.A.H. Russell has said, "There is little doubt that if it were not for the nicotine in tobacco smoke, people would be little more inclined to smoke than they are to blow bubbles or to light sparklers."[71] Former RJR chairman Ross Johnson has even conceded the point. "Of course it's addictive," he said in 1994. "That's why people smoke the stuff."[72] Indeed, as far back as 1527, explorer Bartolomé de Las Casas realized addiction played a role in tobacco use. "I have known Spaniards on the island of Hispaniola, who were accustomed to taking [cigars] and who, being reproved and told that this was a vice, replied that they were not able to stop. . . . I do not know what pleasure or advantage they find in them."[73]

Smoking is truly a powerful addiction—some say it's more addictive than heroin or cocaine. Currently, about 28 percent of Americans smoke, but if all of those who say they want to quit were able to, the smoking rate would plummet to just 7 percent. But quitting is easier wished for than done. Of the 45 million Americans who smoke, each year about 16 million try to kick the habit, but only 1.2 million—that's less than 10 percent of those trying—actually quit.[74]

Smokers who try to quit suffer through the experience, prompting many to quickly take up smoking again. The Surgeon General's report in 1980 outlined several symptoms suffered by smokers trying to quit.

> *When habitual smokers stop smoking, they may experience a wide variety of unpleasant side effects, including craving for tobacco, irritability, restlessness, dullness, sleep disturbance, gastrointestinal disturbances, anxiety and impairment of concentration, judgment and psychomotor performance. . . . Additional objective signs include a decrease in heart rate and blood pressure, increased rapid eye movement sleep, and slower rhythms in the EEG. Spontaneous jaw clenching lasting several weeks has been correlated with verbal reports of irritability.[75]*

The smoking experience is so powerful that former smokers find they still miss the habit years after quitting. The late President Lyndon B. Johnson was a former smoker. "I've missed it every day, but I haven't gone back on it, and I'm glad that I haven't," he said shortly after the first Surgeon General's report on smoking.[76] Interestingly, he started smoking again the day he left office. In his bid to quit smoking, author Richard Klein wrote *Cigarettes Are Sublime*, a tribute to the joys of smoking. "It is not the utility of cigarettes, however useful they may be, that explains their power to attract the undying allegiance of billions of people dying from their habit," Klein wrote. "Rather, the quality that explains their enormous power of seduction is linked to the specific forms of beauty they foster.... The sublimity of cigarettes explains why people love what tastes nasty and makes them sick...."[77]

In his novel *Confessions of Zeno*, Italian writer Italo Svevo tells about a man who spends his entire life trying to quit smoking, constantly promising himself that each cigarette he smokes will be his last.

> *My days became filled with cigarettes and resolutions to give up smoking, and, to make a clean sweep of it, that is more or less what they are still. The dance of the last cigarette which began when I was twenty has not reached its last figure yet. My resolutions are less drastic and, as I grow older, I become more indulgent to my weaknesses. When one is old one can afford to smile at life and all it contains. I may as well say that for some time past I have been smoking a great many cigarettes and have given up calling them the last.*[78]

Yet despite a number of new smoking-cessation products that have been developed in recent years, nothing has emerged that is a true substitute for the smoking experience. Most smoking-cessation products are simply alternative delivery devices for nicotine. They come in the form of patches, gum, nasal spray, and inhalers.

These products help ease nicotine withdrawal symptoms, but they lack the potency of a cigarette, which delivers a rapid and more effective nicotine dose. When a smoker inhales, within seconds the nicotine enters the lungs and travels directly to the brain. Studies show that 80 percent of would-be quitters try to do it "cold turkey," but only about 7 percent succeed. Smokers who seek help from clinics or by using cessation drugs fair better, posting a 15 percent success rate. The average quitter tries to kick the habit six to eight times before finally succeeding.

The most recent advance in stop-smoking aids is a pill, Zyban, a repackaged version of the antidepressant Wellbutrin, which was approved for use as a stop-smoking aid by the FDA in 1997. Zyban doesn't contain nicotine but instead manipulates brain chemicals that are associated with addiction. In 1999, smokers spent $730 million on smoking-cessation products such as patches and gums. In clinical studies, 35 percent of smokers who used Zyban plus a nicotine patch were able to quit. But doctors say the real-world success rate is closer to 15 percent. Yet none of these methods boasts better than a 50 percent long-term success rate.

Once people quit smoking, their risk for various diseases plummets to the same levels enjoyed by lifetime nonsmokers. According to the World Health Organization, just one year after a smoker quits the habit, his or her risk of coronary heart disease decreases by 50 percent. Within 15 years, an ex-smoker's relative risk of dying from heart disease approaches that of a nonsmoker. Ten to 14 years after quitting smoking, the risk of mortality from cancer drops to nearly that of those who have never smoked. The relative risks of lung cancer, chronic lung disease, and stroke also decrease, but more slowly.[79]

As former Surgeon General Koop said recently, "Quitting smoking is never as good as not starting to smoke."

6.

Snuffing It Out:
The Future of an Industry

Tobacco is a dirty weed. I like it.
It satisfies no normal need. I like it.
It makes you thin, it makes you lean,
It takes the hair right off your bean.
It's the worst darn stuff I've ever seen.
I like it.

—G. L. HEMMINGER, PENN STATE *FROTH*

Tobacco Foes

It isn't easy being a smoker. Not only must smokers contend with the knowledge that every smoky, delicious puff is taking minutes off their lives, but they are constantly bombarded with paradoxical messages about their habit. Cigarette advertisements and Hollywood movies portray smokers as rebellious hipsters or beautiful people in control of their lives. What they often don't show are the hordes of zealous antismokers waiting in the wings, ready to flap away at the offending stench of cigarette smoke and lecture about the dangers of secondhand smoke. Smokers, banned from lighting up in most workplaces, restaurants, airports, and public

buildings around the country, now are forced to huddle on side-
walks and outside building doors, inhaling a few quick puffs
before skulking back to the office or dinner table only to be
admonished by disapproving glances from their coworkers and
friends.

Antismoking crusaders are no longer just an American phenomenon either. Many cities in Europe, once bastions of smoking
tolerance, have enacted antismoking laws in public places. In
Japan, marketers sell spritzes to eliminate smoke smells, and stores
sell suits made of smoke-repellant fabrics. Increasingly, smokers
around the world are becoming outcasts. But the conflict between
those who smoke and those who don't isn't a modern-day phenomenon. From the earliest days after explorers in the Americas
discovered this novel "Indian" habit, smoking has ignited controversy.

The origins of the antitobacco movement date back to the
1600s in England, when smoking became a fashionable pastime,
particularly among wealthy young men in London. These smoking "dandies," as they came to be known, smoked with such pomp
and affectation that they are blamed for triggering some of the earliest antismoking sentiments. Smoking opponents quickly divided
into two camps—those who placed tobacco in the category of
liquor, lust, and other wanton behaviors, and those who believed
the plant had medicinal benefits and, like other drugs, shouldn't
be used for pleasure.

In 1602, the first known attack on smokers arrived in the
form of a pamphlet called "Work for Chimney Sweeps." Written
under a pseudonym, the author outlined the reasons for shunning
tobacco, including claims that it caused sterility and made the
brain "sooty," to the belief that it was a product of the devil, not
to be used by "us Christians." The pamphlet was quickly answered
by another pamphlet, "A Defence of Tobacco," by physician Roger
Marbecke. "Me think it were a more charitable notion to think
that it came from God, who is the author of all good gifts, than

from the devil," he wrote. The lines between smokers and non-smokers had been drawn.[1]

The most powerful antitobacco crusader of the time was King James I (1603–1625), whose "Counter Blaste to Tobacco," issued anonymously in 1604, blasted the "stinking" habit. King James was centuries ahead of his time, noting that smoking was an addictive, foul-smelling habit that did terrible things to the inside of the body, particularly the lungs. He noted that smokers spent small fortunes on tobacco and became irritable when they couldn't smoke. He was perhaps the first critic of secondhand smoke and even recognized the role of peer pressure and fashion in encouraging smoking. He accused tobacco users of committing moral sin, comparing smoking to lust and drunkenness. In words laced with sarcasm, he mocked claims that tobacco had medicinal benefits. And, in an uncanny foreshadowing of events to come, the king later imposed a 4,000 percent tax on tobacco in a bid to stamp out smoking. He also sponsored the first-known public debate, held at Oxford University in 1605, on the use of tobacco.

> Surely in my opinion, there cannot be a more base, and yet hurtfull corruption in a country, than is the vile use (or other abuse) of taking tobacco in this kingdom. . . . [C]onsider what honor or policy can move us to imitate the barbarous and beastly manners of the wild, godless, and slavish Indians, especially in so vile and stinking a custom? . . . Shall we, I say, without blushing, abase ourselves so far, as to imitate these beastly Indians, slaves to the Spaniards, refuse to the world, and as yet aliens to the holy Covenant of God? Why do we not as well imitate them in walking naked as they do in preferring glasses, feathers and such toys, to gold and precious stones, as they do? Yea why do we not deny God and adore the Devil, as they do?
>
> . . . Such is the miraculous omnipotency of our strong taste tobacco, as it cures all sorts of diseases (which never any drug

could do before) in all persons, and at all times. It cures all maner of distellations, either in the head or stomach (if you believe their axioms) although in very deed it does both corrupt the brain, and by causing over-quick digestion, fill the stomach full of crudities.... It makes a man sober that was drunk. It refreshes a weary man, and yet makes a man hungry. Being taken when they go to bed, it makes one sleep soundly, and yet being taken when a man is sleepy and drowsy, it will, as they say, awake his brain, and quicken his understanding. As for curing of the Pockes, it serves for that use but among the pockie Indian slaves. Here in England it is refined, and will not deign to cure here any other than cleanly and gentlemanly diseases. Omnipotent power of Tobacco!...

... Many in this kingdom have had such a continual use of taking this unsavory smoke, as now they are not able to forbear the same, no more than an old drunkard can abide to be sober, without falling into an uncurable weakness and evil consitution.... Now how you are by this custom disabled in your goods, let the gentry of this land bear witness, some of them bestowing three, some four hundred pounds a year upon this precious stink, which I am sure might be bestowed upon many far better uses....

... And as for the vanities committed in this filthy custom, is it not both great vanity and uncleanliness that at the table, a place of respect, of cleanliness, of modesty, men should not be ashamed to sit tossing of tobacco pipes and puffing of the smoke of tobacco one to another, making the filthy smoke and stink thereof, to exhale at the dishes and infect the air, when very often men that abhor it are at their repast? Surely smoke becomes a kitchen far better than a dining chamber. And yet it makes a kitchen ... in the inward parts of men, soiling and infecting them with an unctious and oily kind of soot as has been found in some great tobacco takers, that after their death were opened. And not only meat time, but no other time or action is exempted

King James the I.

His Seal & Autograph from the Original in the Possession of John Thane.

King James I
(courtesy of New York Public Library)

from the public use of this uncivil trick.... The public use whereof, at all times and in all places, has now so far prevailed as diverse men very sound in both judgment and complexion have been forced to take it also without desire, partly because they were ashamed to seem singular...and partly to be as one that was content to eat garlic, which he did not love, that he might not be troubled with the smell of it in the breath of his fellows.... But here is not only a great vanity, but a great contempt of God's good gifts, that the sweetness of a man's breath,

being a good gift of God, should be willfully corrupted by this
stinking smoke. . . . Moreover, which is a great inequity and
against all humanity, the husband shall not be ashamed to re-
duce his delicate, wholesome and clean complexioned wife to
that extremety, that either she must also corrupt her sweet breath
or else resolve to live in a perpetual stinking torment. Have you
no reason then to be ashamed, and to forbear this filthy novelty,
so basely grounded, so foolishly received and so grossly mistaken
in the right use thereof? . . .A custom loathesome to the eye,
hateful to the nose, harmful to the brain, dangerous to the lungs
and the black stinking fume thereof, nearest resembling the hor-
rible Stigian smoke of the pit that is bottomless.[2]

But the earnest king's words fell on smoke-filled ears. Tobacco use rapidly increased during his reign, proving an axiom of smoking and authority that is still true today. The more the government protests tobacco, the more the populace wants to smoke it.

The king, however, is hardly a poster child for the antismoking movement. His hatred of the habit wasn't so much driven by any moral or medical concerns but by the fact that he didn't like Raleigh and because his enemies, the Spaniards, controlled much of the world's tobacco trade. Years later, when it became clear that tobacco represented vast revenues for his kingdom, the king's antismoking stance waned. Nonetheless, his "Counter Blaste" rippled through England and across the continent and even into Asia, setting the tone of antitobacco activism for centuries to follow.

Rulers in Europe and Asia often opposed the use of tobacco on moral or religious grounds. But in some places, particularly the Middle East, the dislike of tobacco was fueled by a fear that something so popular from a foreign country was potentially subversive. There were also practical reasons for the tobacco bans: Smoking was a fire hazard and tobacco farms used land needed to grow food crops.

In the early to mid-1600s, the backlash against smoking

turned bloody in many countries, particularly those in the Middle East and Asia. In Japan, smokers and tobacco planters faced confiscation of their property and imprisonment. In China, tobacco traffickers were decapitated. In 1617, the Mogul emperor of Hindustan ordered that smokers should have their lips slit. At about the same time, Murad IV in Turkey and his brother Shah Abbas in Persia outlawed smoking with deadly consequences. In Turkcy, the stem of a pipe was thrust through the nose of a smoker, and he was paraded through the streets on a mule. Other smokers were beheaded or hanged with a pipe driven through their noses. In Persia, tobacco traders lost their noses and ears, while soldiers who smoked had their noses and lips cut off. One tobacco salesman was burned at the stake in a pyre of the tobacco leaves he had hoped to sell. Foreign merchants smoking in a tavern suffered particularly brutal consequences: molten lead was poured down their throats. In Russia, torture, exile to Siberia, and death were ordered for smokers. One smoker was even sent to be consumed by a tribe of cannibals, but, reportedly, he escaped.

Despite these painfully compelling reasons not to smoke, the habit, amazingly, continued to spread. And as it did, governments in Europe, Asia, and even the American colonies soon realized the economic potential of this plant for which smokers were, quite literally, willing to die. Tobacco was brown gold to their cash-strapped treasuries, and the revenues from tobacco import and export taxes quickly convinced many rulers to ease their opposition to the now-lucrative weed. By the end of the seventeenth century, much of the official government opposition to tobacco had waned. In 1725, the pope even allowed snuff use in St. Peter's church, and the Vatican later opened its own tobacco factory.[3]

The invention of the match in 1827 reignited the popularity of smoking, which in turn triggered a new wave of opposition to tobacco. Queen Victoria required her guests to exhale tobacco smoke into fireplaces, while German smokers were fined for smoking in the street. In the United States, the fight against smoking was closely aligned with the temperance movement—indeed, indulgence in tobacco was believed to prompt a craving for "strong drinks."

But the real antitobacco battle began when cigarettes came into fashion in the late 1800s. With smoking rates surging as cigarettes became a mass-produced product, tobacco's foes turned up the heat. The modern fight against the cigarette began with a battle to prevent children from smoking. By 1890, 26 U.S. states had banned sales of cigarettes to minors, and educators noted that truants and juvenile delinquents were almost always smokers.[4] Several states banned cigarette sales altogether, although smokers found ways to obtain their vice by mail order or by crossing state lines. In 1914, Henry Ford, the automobile inventor, joined the crusade against cigarettes, banning cigarettes from his factories. He published a pamphlet, "The Case Against the Little White Slaver," which claimed: "If you study the history of almost any criminal you will find that he is an inveterate cigarette smoker."[5] Inventor Thomas Edison smoked cigars and chewed tobacco, but joined the fight against cigarettes. "I employ no person who smokes cigarettes," he wrote.[6]

Nonsmokers also began to complain about secondhand smoke. In 1904, *Harper's Weekly* criticized smoking manners. "The men who bring lighted cigars into street-cars and smoke in the face of every passenger who crowds past them to get on or off, clearly and scandalously disregard the rights of others."[7]

But the advent of World War I distracted the country and served to stifle the antismoking movement at a time when states began lifting their ban on cigarette sales. In 1925, the *American Mercury* magazine declared "The Triumph of the Cigarette," astutely observing, "The more violently the cigarette has been attacked, the more popular it has become."[8]

Over the next thirty years, the antitobacco forces remained relatively quiet, although the first concerns about the health effects of cigarettes began trickling out of the medical establishment. But the

Smoking Rates in the United States, 1965–2000

YEAR	PERCENTAGE OF SMOKERS
1965	42.4
1966	42.6
1970	37.4
1974	37.1
1978	34.1
1979	33.5
1980	33.2
1983	32.1
1985	30.1
1987	28.8
1988	28.1
1990	25.5
1991	25.7
1992*	26.5
1993	25.0
2000	28.0

*Estimates since 1992 data include sometime smokers

SOURCE: U.S. Department of Health and Human Services.

release of the 1964 Surgeon General's report breathed new life into the anticigarette movement and triggered a new wave of antitobacco sentiments as well as legislation and litigation. Around the country, a series of stop-smoking initiatives were put in place. In 1973, the Civil Aeronautics Board restricted smoking on airlines, making it the first federal restriction on smoking in public places. The same year, Arizona became the first state to pass a comprehensive law restricting smoking in public places. The following year, the town of Monticello, Minnesota, stopped smoking for a day, an event that led to the first Great American Smoke-Out in 1977.[9]

The antismoking efforts snowballed around the country, and today there are few public places that allow smoking. It's now banned in many restaurants, office buildings, and even sports stadiums. Smokers are relegated to bar areas, smoking rooms, and, often, outside.

The antismoking efforts did more than inconvenience smokers. The crackdown on smoking, coupled with the growing body of medical evidence suggesting that smoking caused cancer and other major health problems, resulted in a fast decline in smoking rates. While more than half the population smoked in the 1950s, today that number has plunged to just 28 percent of the adult population.[10] [See Fig. 17]

Blowing the Whistle

While opposition to smoking is as old as the cigarette itself, it wasn't until the 1950s that antismoking sentiments were transformed into a legal assault on the cigarette business. In 1954, the first of more than 1,000 lawsuits blaming Kools, Marlboros, Camels, and Lucky Strikes for a variety of deadly lung and heart ailments was filed, triggering a "first wave" of litigation against the tobacco companies. Even though at the time, the industry's own research showed a strong link between smoking and disease, the cigarette makers resolved to never settle any lawsuit, fearful that any concession would open the floodgates of litigation. In many respects, the first wave of cigarette suits were garden-variety product liability cases—consumers (smokers) were accusing a big corporation (cigarette makers) of making and selling a faulty product (the cigarette). The cigarette was faulty, lawyers argued, because, if used in accordance with manufacturers' instructions (place it in the mouth, light it, inhale), it could make you sick or even kill you.

But Big Tobacco changed the rules of conventional tort litigation. Smoking, tobacco lawyers argued, was a matter of personal choice. And by 1964 smokers had been warned of the risks by no less than the Surgeon General of the United States. As a result, cigarette makers argued that they shouldn't be held liable for the voluntary, personal decisions of smokers. And lest that argument fall short of the mark, tobacco companies hedged their bets by simply wearing down their opponents. A single lawyer, or even an entire law firm, was no match for the militia of lawyers and experts hired by the tobacco companies. Any doubt that Big Tobacco's legal strategy hinged on exhausting its opponents was erased in 1988, when a confidential memo from an R.J. Reynolds lawyer surfaced. "The aggressive posture we have taken regarding depositions and discovery in general continues to make these cases extremely burdensome and expensive to plaintiffs' lawyers, particularly sole practitioners," wrote RJR attorney J. Michael Jordan. "To paraphrase General Patton, the way we won these cases was not by spending all of Reynolds' money, but by making that other son of a bitch spend all his."[11]

And so it went for more than thirty years. Despite reams of scientific evidence, hundreds of thousands of victims, and plenty of experts willing to testify against cigarette manufacturers, tobacco companies never paid a dime in damages. The family of one smoker, 50-year-old carpenter Nathan Horton, who had smoked Pall Malls for 30 years and died of lung cancer, actually won its case in 1990, but the jury awarded zero damages.[12] And therein lies another paradox of the cigarette, notes legal scholar Donald W. Garner. "The industry that markets the most dangerous product sold in America is the only industry that has been completely sheltered from the storm of 20th century product liability."[13]

Over the next ten years, tobacco foes would gain strength and their movement gain momentum. In less than a decade, a combination of new legal strategies, duplicitous public appearances by tobacco executives, the emergence of increasingly damaging tobacco industry research, and the most concerted effort against the industry by the U.S. government ever seen would bring Big Tobacco to its knees.

Things began to change for Big Tobacco in the early 1990s in the town of Clarksdale, Mississippi. Clarksdale was, incidentally, the home of the first Marlboro man, Charles Connelly, who later died of lung cancer. It was also home to Michael T. Lewis, a plaintiff's attorney who spent the spring of 1993 watching Jackie Thompson, the mother of his secretary and a longtime smoker, die of heart disease. Riding down a Memphis hospital elevator, the story goes, Mr. Lewis thought about ways to avenge Jackie Thompson's suffering. He knew about the futile efforts of lawyers before him to sue on behalf of smokers, but wondered about the hundreds of thousands of dollars it was costing Medicaid to pay for Mrs. Thompson's care. Mrs. Thompson had chosen to smoke, thought Mr. Lewis, but the taxpayers were unwilling victims because they were now forced to bear the brunt of her habit and subsequent illness. And then it dawned on him. Suing on behalf of these unwilling victims, thought Lewis, could be the way to beat the tobacco companies.

Lewis called on his former classmate, Ole Miss law school grad Michael Moore, who was now state attorney general. Lewis said he simply needed a "reality check." "I was a little worried about the grandiosity and the novelty of it," Lewis told the *Wall Street Journal*. "Because it seemed like if it was such a good idea, someone else would have thought of it besides me."[14]

Attorney General Moore put Lewis in touch with another Ole Miss grad, Richard F. Scruggs, who had made millions in asbestos litigation. Don Barrett, a lawyer from Lexington, Mississippi, who had represented the family of Nathan Horton, and won their case but not any money, also joined the team. The state of Mississippi, the trio discovered, was funding the care for 500,000 Medicaid patients—and 200,000 had smoking-related illnesses.

Even as the Mississippi team was mapping out the new Medicaid strategy, officials in Washington were ready to level their own volley in the Tobacco Wars, triggering a series of events that spiraled into a massive assault on the tobacco industry. David Kessler, Commissioner of the Food and Drug Administration, announced he was investigating allegations that cigarette makers had manipulated nicotine levels in cigarettes in a bid to keep people smoking.[15] Kessler had for some time mulled whether and how the FDA should get involved in the tobacco debate. It was nicotine that intrigued him most. The FDA, after all, regulates nicotine patches and gum as drug-delivery devices, so why not cigarettes?

In February 1994, Dr. Kessler declared his intent to begin regulating nicotine as a drug. Just three days later, the ABC News program *Day One* revealed that it had uncovered the tobacco industry's "last, best secret": that cigarette companies control nicotine levels to keep smokers hooked.[16] Although the report shed light on the methods companies use to control nicotine levels in tobacco, the network made a critical mistake when it made a reference to the "spiking" of tobacco. That, claimed Philip Morris, implied that the industry added additional nicotine to tobacco— the company has said that no nicotine is added beyond what occurs normally in the tobacco plant. Philip Morris sued ABC for $10 billion, and ABC later announced it would settle the case and issue a limited apology for certain claims in the report.[17]

Despite the embarrassment to ABC, the report forever changed the national debate on cigarette smoking. For years the conventional wisdom was that nicotine was a naturally occurring ingredient in tobacco leaves. Now it was known that nicotine, while occurring naturally, was also carefully controlled by cigarette makers.

The FDA announcement and *Day One* report spurred the filing of what came to be known as the Castano case, one of the most significant tobacco lawsuits to date. Wendell Gauthier, a New Orleans attorney who had won millions suing on behalf of plane-crash and hotel-fire victims, had a year earlier lost his long time friend, 47-year-old Peter J. Castano, to lung cancer. Gauthier decided that instead of suing Big Tobacco for the wrongful death of his friend, a suit he was certain to lose, he would sue the industry for his friend's addiction. The industry had warned of the health risks associated with smoking, but they hadn't warned that smoking was addictive. The idea that tobacco companies could control nicotine levels meant that cigarette makers, not individual smokers, were responsible for the addicting habit. Gauthier also realized that the only way to win would be to match Big Tobacco's legal army with an army of his own. He assembled 60 lawfirms who each promised $100,000 annually to fund a national class action on behalf of all addicted smokers.[18]

By the spring of 1994, Representative Henry Waxman, a Democrat from California, chairman of the House Subcommittee on Health and Environment, was holding yet another round of hearings about tobacco. For more than a decade, Waxman had tormented Big Tobacco by holding hearings on a variety of anti-smoking measures, spurring public debate and eking out bits and pieces of information about the shadowy industry. On April 14, 1994, Waxman provided Congress and a national television audience with one of the most memorable moments in the tobacco debate. He summoned the chief executive officers of the nation's seven major tobacco companies to testify before his subcommittee. In the crowded wood-paneled hearing room, the men lined up, side-by-side, with their right hands raised, swearing to tell the truth, the whole truth. A *New York Times* photographer captured the moment but the men didn't look like chief executives. They looked like defendants in a trial.

Waxman and his fellow committee members quizzed the executives about addiction, nicotine, and cancer.

> **Rep. Ron Wyden of Oregon:** Let me ask you first, and I'd like to just go down the row, whether each of you believes that nicotine is not addictive?
>
> **Campbell:** I believe nicotine is not addictive, yes.

Johnston: Congressman, cigarettes and nicotine clearly do not meet the classic definitions of addiction. . . .

Taddeo: I don't believe that nicotine or our products are addicting.

Tisch: I believe nicotine is not addictive.

Horrigan: I believe nicotine is not addictive.

Sandefur: I believe nicotine is not addictive.

Johnson: And I too believe that nicotine is not addictive.[19]

The appearance of the seven executives before Congress would come back to haunt Big Tobacco in more ways than one. Not only would the Justice Department later investigate the executives on allegations of perjury, but the seeming indifference of the executives fueled a growing antitobacco sentiment. Among those watching Big Tobacco's appearance before Congress was Grady Carter, a 66-year-old former air traffic controller who had smoked Lucky Strikes for more than 40 years and now suffered from lung cancer. "I had tried so hard to quit and there they all were saying it wasn't addictive," Carter told the *Wall Street Journal.*[20] As a result of the Waxman hearings, Grady Carter sued Brown & Williamson, maker of Lucky Strikes, in what would later become the most significant lawsuit ever waged by a smoker.

Not long after the tobacco executives testified before Congress, Michael Moore, Mississippi attorney general, marched into the Jackson County court, making Mississippi the first state to sue to recoup the health costs of tobacco-related illnesses. The Mississippi state legislature wouldn't pay for the novel lawsuit, and the state governor opposed the effort, even trying, unsuccessfully, to block it in state supreme court. But Dick Scruggs, the asbestos lawyer, and another attorney, Ron Motley, fronted the cost of the suit, gambling that the return on their investment would come in the form of lucrative contingency fees—if they won. Hoping to put even more pressure on the tobacco companies, Moore began lobbying other state officials to file their own Medicaid reimbursement suits.[21]

But perhaps the biggest turning point in the Tobacco Wars was triggered by two men from the ranks of Big Tobacco itself. In the spring of 1994, a man named Merrell Williams contacted Scruggs, the attorney funding the Mississippi lawsuit. Williams had worked as a paralegal at the lawfirm of Wyatt, Tarrant & Combs in Louisville, Kentucky. He had a patchwork employment history that included jobs as an actor, playwright, college professor, auto importer, waiter, rose cutter, and Irish pub owner. In his $9-an-hour job at the law firm, he catalogued documents filled with tantalizing secrets from Brown & Williamson, which manufactured Kools, the brand Williams himself had smoked for years.[22]

Although he'd been warned—even threatened—to never discuss the documents with outsiders, Williams was intrigued by the reams of secret memos and studies. He pored through documents that revealed that the tobacco company knew cigarettes were addictive as early as 1963. The papers detailed the company's relationship with politicians, lobbyists, and Hollywood film studios. Documents about carcinogenic ingredients, efforts to make a safer cigarette, and even the company's plans to target "starters," people who haven't started smoking, all passed across his desk. Williams had furtively copied many of the documents, hiding them under his clothes.

To this day, Williams says he really doesn't know why he took the documents that have rocked an industry. Like many of the other players in the tobacco debate, smoke has permeated Williams's personal life. His father was a longtime smoker of Lucky Strikes until a heart attack at the age of 52. His sister was disabled by lung disease related to smoking; his mother suffers from congestive heart failure and emphysema and requires an oxygen tank to breath.[23]

Williams couldn't tell his story to the media—the documents, after all, were stolen property. Brown & Williamson quickly won a restraining order that prevented him from discussing his work or releasing the papers. Out of a job and mired in a legal morass with

B&W attorneys, Williams contacted Scruggs, who provided the would-be whistleblower a home, a job, and a sailboat. Tobacco lawyers said it was a payoff; Scruggs said it was charity.[24]

Although the court order preventing the release of the Brown & Williamson documents still held, 4,000 pages were delivered anonymously to antitobacco activist Stanley Glantz at the University of California at San Francisco. The return address read "Mr. Butts," a reference to the animated cigarette that represented the tobacco industry in the *Doonesbury* cartoon strip. The documents also mysteriously appeared on the Internet, and over time, fell into the hands of members of Congress, the media, and antitobacco forces. Nobody has ever admitted to distributing the papers, but the broad dissemination of the material produced the desired result. A judge eventually ruled that the documents were now in the public domain and could no longer be quashed by the courts or B&W.[25]

The release of the papers opened the floodgates against Big Tobacco. They have been used in Congressional hearings and smokers' lawsuits. States seeking to recoup billions in medical costs have relied on these internal memos to prove tobacco companies have long been aware of the dangers of their products. The documents provided a rare glimpse into the internal workings of the tobacco industry, and, as a result, have supported the case for federal regulation of cigarettes and prompted an investigation of tobacco executives for perjury. One document, for instance, was called "A Tentative Hypothesis on Nicotine Addiction," explaining the drug's addictive effects. It was nothing less than a smoking gun. The document was dated 1963, more than 30 years before company executives had testified before Congress that nicotine was *not* addictive.[26]

For his part, Williams, still immersed in a legal quagmire, says he didn't realize what he had started. "I wish it had never happened," he says. "It's been too much grief for me. To repeat this in history is like dying all over again."[27]

About the same time that Williams was seeking refuge with

Scruggs, another man, Jeffrey S. Wigand, was watching the Waxman hearings. Wigand, a former top research executive at Brown & Williamson, has said he was infuriated by the denials of the tobacco industry and decided to break his silence about his former employer. Wigand is Brown & Williamson's former research chief, a $300,000-a-year job, and the tobacco industry's highest-ranking defector. If the documents obtained by Merrell Williams served as a confusing road map of the cigarette business, Wigand emerged as the tour guide, helping plaintiffs' lawyers and government officials to unlock some of the industry's best-kept secrets and to build a case against Big Tobacco.

For months, nobody—including the federal officials working with Wigand—knew who he was. A man known to federal officials only by the code name "Research" met with FDA chief Dr. Kessler to help him decipher some of the purloined B&W documents. Dr. Kessler went down a list of names in the papers, asking Research to identify each executive's role in the company. "Who's Jeff Wigand?" Dr. Kessler asked. "I'm Jeff Wigand," Research answered.[28]

In a now-famous 1995 deposition in Mississippi, Wigand accused former B&W chairman Thomas E. Sandefur of lying to Congress about his views on nicotine addiction. He claimed B&W hid damaging scientific research, quashed efforts to make cigarettes safer, and even continued to use a compound found in rat poison in certain types of pipe tobacco.[29]

In one of the most dramatic moments of the Tobacco Wars, Wigand was asked whether he and B&W executives had ever discussed the addictive nature of nicotine:

A: There have been numerous statements made by a number of officers, particularly Mr. Sandefur, that we're in the nicotine-delivery business.

Q: The nicotine-delivery business?

A: And that tar is nothing but negative baggage. . . .

Later, lawyers argued over how much Mr. Wigand could say about coumarin, a compound sometimes used in both pipe tobaccos and rat poisons.

> **Mr. Motley (for Mississippi):** Sir at any time did you learn that Brown & Williamson was using a form of rat poison in pipe tobacco?
>
> **Mr. Bezanson (for B&W):** Object to form.
>
> **Mr. Wigand:** It is a compound called coumarin. It was contained in the pipe tobacco.
>
> **Mr. Bezanson:** Object on trade secret grounds and instruct not to answer.
>
> **Mr. Motley:** You are objecting that the man is revealing that you used rat poison as a trade secret? You may answer sir.
>
> **Mr. Bezanson:** Object to the form.
>
> **Mr. Motley:** Go ahead. If they used rat poison in pipe tobacco that human beings were taking in their bodies, I want to know about it. Will you tell me about it, sir?
>
> **Mr. Bezanson:** Object to the form.
>
> **Mr. Wigand:** I was concerned about the continued use of coumarin in pipe tobacco after the coumarin had been removed from cigarettes because of the FDA not allowing the use of coumarin in foods with additives. The reason why it stayed in pipe tobacco is the removal would change the taste of the pipe tobacco and, therefore, affect sales.[30]

In 1996 Wigand became a public figure in the tobacco debate after working with the CBS news show *60 minutes* on a story about the secrets of Big Tobacco. Legal wranglings stalled the broadcast, but once the details of Mr. Wigand's depositions were revealed in the press, the show went on. B&W then made the surprising decision to attack Wigand directly, providing the *Wall Street Journal* with a 500-page dossier on his comings and goings, as witnessed by private investigators hired to ferret out his flaws. The headlines in the report included "The Misconduct of Jeffrey S. Wigand Available in the Public Record," "Wigand's Lies about his Residence," "Wigand's Lies Under Oath," and "Other Lies by Wigand."

The strategy backfired, however, when the paper printed a front-page story dissecting the report. The conclusion: "A close look at the file, and independent research by this newspaper into its key claims, indicates that many of the serious allegations against Mr. Wigand are backed by scant or contradictory evidence. Some of the charges—including that he pleaded guilty to shoplifting—are demonstrably untrue."[31]

By the fall of 1995, the growing steam behind the antitobacco efforts hadn't gone unnoticed by lawyers representing Bennett S. LeBow, the financier who controls Liggett Group, the smallest of the big five U.S. tobacco companies and the firm with the slimmest profits. In December 1995, LeBow authorized his lawyers to begin settlement talks.[32]

On March 13, 1996, even as other cigarette makers were vowing to never give in, Liggett reached a widespread settlement. The company agreed to pay 5 percent of its pretax income for 25 years, up to $50 million, as well as publicize its ingredients and put additional warning labels on its packages. The defection of LeBow shifted the balance of power in the tobacco debate. Now antitobacco advocates had one of tobacco's own helping them unearth some of the industry's best-kept secrets. Why did LeBow give in? "Over the years they kept telling me that they were going to win everything and increasingly, I didn't believe a word of it," LeBow told the *Wall Street Journal*. "What was I supposed to do—sit and wait for bankruptcy?"[33]

By August, tobacco stocks were pounded by more bad news. A Jacksonville, Florida, jury had delivered a startling verdict on behalf of Grady Carter, the smoker so miffed by the industry's claims that cigarettes weren't addictive that he sued. A jury awarded Mr. Carter $750,000 in damages, the first time a smoker had won damages in a straight liability suit. The difference this time, jurors said, was a slew of damaging internal company documents that showed the industry had been aware of the hazards of cigarettes since the 1950s.[34] The documents had surfaced as a result of the Mississippi lawsuit.

So by August 1996, Big Tobacco was weathering the most significant assault in the industry's history. President Clinton had endorsed an FDA plan to curb underage smoking, and the agency was hoping to regulate cigarettes as nicotine-delivery devices. The state of Mississippi had come up with an unorthodox approach of suing cigarette makers to recoup medical costs, and two dozen states had filed copycat lawsuits. Another 60 law firms were suing on behalf of addicted smokers, and reams of internal documents had leaked out and fueled the efforts. The industry had suffered its first defeat at the hands of a jury, and had seen one of its own, Liggett Group, capitulate to the mounting pressure.

In September, top tobacco executives began holding secret meetings to consider the unthinkable: settlement. For more than 40 years, the industry had steadfastly held to the belief that it would never settle a smoker's lawsuit and never pay out a dime in damages. So why the dramatic about-face? There was an economic imperative at work: A settlement would shield tobacco companies from the specter of ever-spiraling damage awards. On June 20, 1997, a 68-page settlement proposal emerged. Big Tobacco would agree to pay $368.5 billion over 25 years, curtail tobacco advertising, help curb underage smoking, and issue warning labels declaring cigarettes addictive.[35] What they would get in return was extensive liability protection and provisions that would make it difficult for the FDA to reduce nicotine content in cigarettes. As Congress began debating the measure, additional proposals cropped up, including plans to hike cigarette prices.

The settlement quickly became bogged down in a political debate as several health activists criticized the deal for capitulating to tobacco interests. One provision giving the tobacco companies a massive tax break on money paid in the settlement infuriated the antismoking community. Eventually, the federal settlement failed, but the industry had shifted into a new mode for dealing with its legal troubles. After years of resisting any concession to the antitobacco forces, the industry now realized that settlement was the easiest, fastest way to make its problems go away. Philip Morris, Reynolds, Brown & Williamson, and Lorillard began negotiations with the individual states who had sued them to recover Medicaid costs, and they quickly reached multibillion-dollar settlements with Mississippi, Texas, Florida, and Minnesota for a total of $40 billion. In the fall of 1998, the tobacco giants reached a multistate settlement with the remaining 46 states that either had suits pending against the tobacco industry or had agreed not to sue in exchange for a share of the largess.

On top of direct payments to the states, the tobacco companies promised to fund antismoking campaigns nationwide and pledged another $250 million during the next 10 years to establish a national public health foundation to reduce teen smoking. They also agreed to limited restrictions on tobacco advertising and promotions.[36]

But the settlement with state lawyers doesn't put an end to Big Tobacco's troubles. More than 400 individual lawsuits against the industry are still pending around the United States. To be sure, the cigarette companies have in the past had remarkable success in swatting down lawsuits against them. But recent history shows that the industry is becoming increasingly vulnerable to a number of new legal arguments that focus on the addictive nature of cigarettes as well as the cigarette industry's efforts to win new smokers by targeting children. And as public hostility toward the industry grows amid revelations that cigarette makers have long known that smoking is both addictive and can lead to cancer, the cigarette industry faces an increasingly hostile jury pool in court.

As a result, cigarette makers now fully expect to lose some of the cases brought by individual smokers. What isn't yet clear is whether cigarette companies will begin losing more than they win.

The $750,000 Grady Carter verdict, for instance, has since been overturned by an appeals court. Following a shocking $50 million judgment by a California jury, Philip Morris lawyer William Ohlemeyer notes that changing demographics and attitudes about smoking are changing the rules of cigarette litigation. "The jury pool is getting younger," he says. "The environment the cases are being tried in has changed, partly because of the decline in the social acceptance of smoking" in younger age groups.[37]

But while the cigarette makers may be rethinking their defense strategy, don't expect them to give up the fight. Fighting a tobacco case takes time and money—and most sick smokers don't have much of either one. The industry, on the other hand, has plenty of lawyers on the clock and money to burn.

When the Smoke Clears

So have we heard the death knell for the cigarette? The Tobacco Wars have left the cigarette manufacturers bruised and battered, and a seemingly endless legal battle looms both in the United States and in international markets. But rather than representing an end to the cigarette business, the recent legal wranglings, settlements, and jury verdicts signal a new and even promising era for cigarettes and the industry that creates them.

While revelations about industry shenanigans and efforts to cover up the addictive nature of tobacco certainly has fueled hostility toward the cigarette, the emergence of those once-secret documents has also served to defuse the debate. For years, health crusaders focused much of their energy on uncovering wrongdoing by the industry. Now that they've succeeded, the settlement with tobacco has taken much of the steam out of the antitobacco movement.

By forcing the industry's misdeeds out into the open, the anticigarette lobby has, in effect, allowed the cigarette makers to move on and leave much of their wrongdoing behind them. And by settling the cases brought by the states, the cigarette makers have effectively taken away an important platform used by the antitobacco community. State leaders have stopped staging press conferences and political speeches railing against the industry— they've proven their point and have themselves moved on to other issues. To be sure, the reams of industry documents that have surfaced will continue to haunt the tobacco industry in court for years. But over time, it will simply become an accepted part of tobacco's past that it once lied and covered up and misled when it came to the health consequences of cigarettes. But at some point, the industry will get a clean slate, a fresh start. In 20 years, what smoker will legitimately be able to claim that he or she didn't know cigarettes were harmful or addictive? And how shocked will a jury really be when it hears that a tobacco executive in the 1960s knew about the addictive nature of cigarettes? It will be yesterday's news.

Even more startling is the fact that tobacco companies and health crusaders are now partners across the United States. For the first time, tobacco executives and antitobacco forces are linked monetarily. Scores of health programs around the country are now dependent on millions and millions of funds provided by the tobacco companies as a result of the state settlement. Much of the money is being used to fund antismoking campaigns aimed at children, which now appears to be the primary focus of the antitobacco movement. But there's no real evidence that telling kids not to smoke really works. Indeed, studies have shown that it can often have the opposite effect. Children, by their very nature, love to defy authority, and spending millions on advertising to vilify the cigarette could ultimately serve to enhance its appeal. The cigarette is and will continue to be forbidden fruit.

Tobacco companies have also promised to wage their own antismoking campaigns aimed at children and teenagers, but this, too, has not been without controversy. Antitobacco crusaders see the industry's funding of stop-smoking campaigns as a public relations effort that will ultimately thwart more meaning-ful attempts to curb teen smoking. Christopher Buckley lam-pooned this issue in his satire, *Thank You For Smoking*. He writes about a tobacco lobbyist named Nick who, in an effort to win public favor, has promised millions of dollars toward an anti-smoking campaign. He rejects the first campaign proposed by the ad agency because it is effective, and instead asks for a "turkey."

"Okay," Nick said to Sven, who was staring back at him on the video-phone, "does it gobble?" . . .

"What we did was to take the 'Some People Want You to Smoke. We Don't' concept, which avoided the whole health issue, and instead tapped into the adolescent's innate fear of being manipulated by adults. You didn't like it."

"Right. Because it was effective."

"It's gone. So now we're going to be blunt, we want to speak to them with the voice of despised authority, nag them, tell them to go to their rooms, turn them completely off."

"I like it already," Nick said.

"Okay," Sven said. "Here we go." He pulled the board into video camera range. All it had on it was type. It said, "Everything Your Parents Told You About Smoking Is Right."

"Hmm," Nick said.

"You know what I love about it?" Sven said. "It's dullness."

"It is dull," Nick admitted.

"It's deadly. Kids are probably going to look at this and go, 'Puuke.' "

That would probably be Joey's reaction, Nick mused.

"And yet," Sven said, "its brilliance, if I may say so, is in its deconstructability."

"How's that?"

"Say the last three words out loud."

"Smoking Is Right."

"Gobbles on the outside, grabs you on the inside. A Trojan turkey."

"I think," Nick said, "that I can sell this to my people."[38]

The cigarette business does face one serious and still uncertain hurdle—government regulation. But even a heavily regulated tobacco industry will continue to churn out cigarettes. And as long as they are churning out cigarettes, they will sell them, consumers will buy them, and people will continue to smoke. And if people keep smoking, the cigarette makers will continue to make money.

"What have these public health people achieved in 40 years?" asked Steven F. Goldstone, chairman of RJR Nabisco, in a 1998 interview in the *New York Times Magazine.* "They think they'll end smoking by bankrupting us, but believe me, that's not going to happen."[39]

And even if, in a worst-case scenario, the burden of the U.S. Tobacco Wars ultimately sends one or more of the cigarette makers into bankruptcy, cigarettes won't be stubbed out. Out of the ashes, a new cigarette maker will arise—perhaps with a different name and brands, but without the liabilities of the past. The new company very likely would emerge stronger and more profitable than its predecessor.

Meanwhile, most believe it will be years before the rest of the world reaches the same level of antitobacco fervor so prevalent in the United States. Even now, the tobacco road leads to the emerging economies of eastern Europe and Southeast Asia. And China, that Holy Grail of cigarette marketing, beckons. It's widely believed that over the next several years, the Chinese government will loosen its grip on that market, opening it up to Western cigarette marketers. And remember what anticigarette activist Judith MacKay said, as quoted earlier in these pages? "If any cigarette company could capture the China market, it wouldn't matter if every smoker in North America quit tomorrow."

Cigarettes for Sale in Shanghai
(© Bojan Brecelj/Corbis)

And what of the industry's liability abroad? Tobacco companies are just beginning to get a handle on the legal battle the industry faces in other countries. Individual smokers around the world are seeking damages from cigarette makers, but it's less clear whether the industry will be required to reach settlements in other countries similar to the one that it reached with states in the United States. Indeed, the outlook so far looks promising for the industry. A federal judge in Washington, D.C., has dismissed a suit waged by Guatemala to recover its costs from treating sick smokers. Guatemala was the first foreign government to sue the industry, and several other countries, including Venezuela, Bolivia, Nicaragua, and Ukraine have brought similar suits, but the judge's ruling brings that effort to a screeching halt. The court ruled that the injuries alleged by the government of Guatemala were not closely enough connected to the cigarette makers to claim damages. The only way for such health-cost claims to proceed, courts have ruled in similar cases in the United States, is on behalf of individual smokers, one at a time. Given the cost and time such claims would take, it's unlikely anyone will be able to pursue them.[40]

To be sure, there will be setbacks. The industry likely will lose an occasional legal battle and continue to be vilified by antitobacco forces. But history has shown that the attacks on the industry tend to come in waves. Most industry observers agree that while some uncertainties remain, the worst is probably over. The state cases were settled without bankrupting the industry. Criminal investigations into the actions of tobacco executives have ended with no indictments. The Supreme Court has ruled that the Food and Drug Administration doesn't have jurisdiction over cigarettes. Two dozen class-action suits by smokers have been rejected by the courts. And although the industry has lost a few cases brought by individual smokers, the reality is that very few plaintiffs' attorneys are still willing to pursue smokers' claims. They are complicated, expensive, and time-consuming and a payday is far from a sure thing.

What often gets lost in the flurry of news reports about tobacco's woes is the fact that the cigarette makers are making money—lots and lots of it. In 1999, RJR sold $7.56 billion worth of tobacco in the U.S. alone, a 33 percent jump over the previous year. Philip Morris's U.S. tobacco sales jumped 28 percent to $19.6 billion during the same period.

As BAT chief executive Martin Broughton said after divesting the company's insurance arm, tobacco is a good business to be in. "The message is that we are a tobacco company, and that we will invest in tobacco and believe it can be an attractive industry," he said.[41]

Indeed, it's easy to focus on the trouble the Tobacco Wars have created for the cigarette business, but, as former RJR chief Goldstone pointed out, what has really been accomplished? In the U.S., the epicenter of the industry's legal troubles, the slide in tobacco use has stalled and consumption has hovered around 28 percent for several years. Of course, 50 million smokers have stopped smoking, but another 50 million continue to puff away and youth smoking is on the rise. "The industry has been confronted with a variety of tax, regulatory, legal and public policy challenges for 50 years," says Morgan Stanley analyst David Adelman. "The cumulative impact of those factors has been very manageable."

And now, with their worst secrets out in the open, the tobacco industry has been freed to stake out a middle ground. They have conceded that smoking is bad for you, and that it is addictive. While it sounds humble, it is also smart. Staking out the middle makes tobacco critics look like extremists. In addition, admitting that their products are risky allows the industry to freely pursue that so far elusive—yet potentially lucrative—quest for a "safe" cigarette.

In a particularly conciliatory performance, Philip Morris USA chief executive Michael Szymanczyk recently told Florida jurors that the company is mending its ways. "It was pretty clear what Philip Morris was doing was out of alignment with society's expectations of it," he told the jury.[42]

The fact remains that smoking is an intrinsic part of modern culture. For 500 years, smokers and tobacco makers have risked torture and even death at the hands of tobacco's enemies, so it's unlikely that a bunch of lawyers and politicians and the looming threat of deadly disease will fell either the industry or the habit. When the smoke clears from the Tobacco Wars, the last man (or woman) standing may well be a smoker with a cigarette in his (or her) mouth.

Notes on Sources

I've heard it said that journalists, by definition, are "beachcombers on the shores of other people's wisdom." In compiling this book, I have relied heavily on the wisdom of others as chronicled in a wide number of articles and books. The most exhaustive and complete account of the history and scope of the tobacco business is Richard Kluger's *Ashes to Ashes*. It is an exceptional book and a must-read for anyone interested in the tobacco industry. Jerome Brooks's introduction to the Arents Collection at the New York Public Library provides a widely quoted essay on the early history of the industry. Philip Hilts's *Smokescreen* offers a dramatic and riveting account of the industry's research and subsequent cover-up of the health consequences of smoking. The most extraordinary book I came across in my research was David Krogh's *Smoking: The Artificial Passion*, an exploration of both the physical and psychological reasons that cause people to smoke. It is, even for nonsmokers, a fascinating study in human behavior.

I also relied heavily on the published works of several longtime tobacco reporters, particularly the work of Suein Hwang and Alix Freedman of the *Wall Street Journal*. I owe a special thanks to Suein for her moral support and guidance throughout this project. The story of tobacco's foray into new markets has been told best by the *Washington Post*'s Glenn Frankel, while the work of reporters at the Greensboro, N.C., *News & Record* provided insights into the plight of tobacco workers in the United States.

Longtime tobacco industry analysts David Adelman of Morgan Stanley Dean Witter and Gary Black of Sanford C. Benstein & Associates helped me decipher the economics of the industry. This book is filled with data and statistics from Euromonitor's *World Tobacco Report*. Finally, all research into tobacco must begin and end at Gene Borio's amazingly comprehensive Tobacco BBS web site, www.tobacco.org. It is a virtual road map of the tobacco business and was an invaluable tool in my research.

Selected Bibliography

Buckley, Christopher. *Thank You for Smoking*. New York: Random House, 1995.

Burrough, Bryan, and John Helyar. *Barbarians at the Gate: The Fall of RJR Nabsico*. New York: Harper & Row, 1990.

Corina, Maurice. *Trust in Tobacco: The Story of the Men and the Events that Created the Great Tobacco Companies*. New York: St. Martin's, 1975.

Ewen, Stuart. *PR! A Social History of Spin*. New York: Basic Books, 1996.

Glantz, Stanton; Slade, John; Bero, Lisa A.; Hanauer, Peter; and Barnes, Deborah E. *The Cigarette Papers*. Berkeley, Calif.: University of California Press, 1998.

Hilts, Philip J. *Smokescreen: The Truth Behind the Tobacco Industry Coverup*. Reading, Mass.: Addison-Wesley, 1996.

Klein, Richard. *Cigarettes Are Sublime*. Durham and London: Duke University Press, 1993.

Kluger, Richard. *Ashes to Ashes: America's Hundred Year Cigarette War, the Public Health, and the Unabashed Triumph of Philip Morris*. New York: Alfred A. Knopf, 1996.

Krogh, David. *Smoking: The Artificial Passion*. Oxford: W. H. Freeman & Co., 1991.

Kufrin, Joan. *Leo Burnett, Star Reacher*. Chicago: Leo Burnett Co., 1995.

Petrone, Gerard S. *Tobacco Advertising: The Great Seduction*. Atglen, Penn.: Schiffer Publishing, 1996.

Pringle, Peter. *Cornered: Big Tobacco at the Bar of Justice*. New York: Henry Holt & Co, 1998.

Robert, Joseph C. *The Story of Tobacco in America*. Chapel Hill: University of North Carolina Press, 1949, 1967.

Taylor, Peter. *The Smoke Ring: Tobacco, Money and Multinational Politics*. New York: Pantheon Books, 1984.

Stauber, John, and Sheldon Rampton. *Toxic Sludge Is Good For You! Lies, Damn Lies and the Public Relations Industry*. Monroe, Maine: Common Courage Press, 1995.

Sullum, Jacob. *For Your Own Good: The Anti-Smoking Crusade and the Tyranny of Public Health*. New York: The Free Press, 1998.

Tennant, Richard B. *The American Cigarette Industry: A Study in Economic Analysis and Public Policy*. Archon Books, 1971.

Tilley, Nannie M. *The R.J. Reynolds Tobacco Co*. Chapel Hill and London: University of North Carolina Press, 1985.

Notes

PREFACE

1. Philip J. Hilts, *Smokescreen: The Truth Behind the Tobacco Industry Cover-up* (Reading, Mass: Addison-Wesley, 1996), 65. According to the Campaign for Tobacco-Free Kids, most smokers began smoking as children. The average youth smoker begins at age thirteen and becomes a daily smoker by age fourteen and a half. Much of the data on kids and smoking comes from the Robert Wood Johnson Foundation Survey, "Results of a National Household Survey to Assess Public Attitudes About Policy Alternatives for Limiting Minor's Access to Tobacco Products," December, 1994.

2. Federal Trade Commission, *Report to Congress for 1996 Pursuant to the Federal Cigarette Labeling and Advertising Act* (Washington, D.C.: Federal Trade Commission, 1998).

3. David Krogh, *Smoking: The Artificial Passion* (Oxford: W. H. Freeman, 1991), 3.

4. Euromonitor PLC, *World Market for Tobacco* (London: Euromonitor PLC, 1997, 2000).

CHAPTER ONE

1. Euromonitor PLC, *World Market for Tobacco* (London: Euromonitor PLC, 1997, 2000).

2. Bob Newhart, "Introducing Tobacco to Civilization." Used by permission.

3. Jerome E. Brooks, *The Library Relating to Tobacco Collected by George Arents* (New York: New York Public Library, 1937),143.

4. Maurice Corina, *Trust in Tobacco: The Story of the Men and the Events that Created the Great Tobacco Companies* (New York: St. Martin's, 1975), 24–26.

5. Corina, 65.

6. Corina, 117.

7. Richard Kluger, *Ashes to Ashes: America's Hundred Year Cigarette War, the Public Health, and the Unabashed Triumph of Philip Morris* (New York: Alfred A. Knopf, 1996), 56–57.

8. United States Department of Agriculture (USDA), *Total and Per Capita Manufactured Cigarette Consumption, 1900–1995* (Washington, D.C.: United States Department of Agriculture).

9. Kluger, 63.

10. Richard Klein, *Cigarettes Are Sublime* (Durham and London: Duke University Press, 1993), 139–141.

11. Kluger, 63.

12. USDA.

13. Kluger, 113.

14. Kluger, 117.

15. Kluger, 64.

16. USDA.

17. Joseph C. Robert, *The Story of Tobacco in America* (Chapel Hill: University of North Carolina Press, 1949, 1967), 269.

18. From a speech by Cornell University Professor Richard Klein at the New School University forum "Cigarette Seduction," New York, Feb. 5, 1998.

19. David Krogh, *Smoking: The Artificial Passion* (Oxford: W. H. Freeman, 1991), 103.

20. Krogh, 15.

21. Centers for Disease Control, Office on Smoking and Health, "Tobacco Use—United States, 1900–1999," *Morbidity and Mortality Weekly Report*, Nov. 5, 1999, p. 986. According to the CDC, tobacco use among high school seniors fell to about 30% in the late 1970s to the mid-1980s, but increased to 36.5% between 1991 and 1997. Prevalence among high school seniors today is highest among whites and lowest among blacks.

22. Donald Gould, *New Scientist*, April 3, 1976.

CHAPTER TWO

1. American Economics Group, *The U.S. Tobacco Industry in 1994: Its Economic Impact in the States* (Washington, D.C.: American Economics Group, 1996).

2. Federal Trade Commission, *Report to Congress for 1996 Pursuant to the Federal Cigarette Labeling and Advertising Act* (Washington D.C.: Federal Trade Commission, 1998).

3. *Advertising Age*, "Inside Line: Sponsorship Spending Will Reach 8.7 billion," Jan. 24, 2000.

4. The Staff of the *Wall Street Journal*, *Wall Street Journal Almanac* (New York: Ballantine Books, 1999).

5. Tobacco Institute, *The Tax Burden on Tobacco* (Washington D.C.: Tobacco Institute, 1997).

6. Centers for Disease Control.

7. National Fire Protection Association, "1991–1995 NFIRS and NFPA Survey," Quincy, Mass.

8. For the 12 months ending April 2000, the sales of over-the-counter cessation products were about $580 million according to Information Resources Incorporated of Chicago. Sales of prescription cessation drugs for the same period were about $154 million, according to pharmaceutical firm IMS Health of Plymouth Meeting, Penn.

9. Yumiko Ono, "If Cigarette Industry Coughs, Remote Areas Expect to Catch Cold," *Wall Street Journal*, October 26, 1995.

10. World Health Organization, "The Smoking Epidemic: A Fire in the Global Village," August 25, 1997.

11. From a speech by former U.S. Surgeon General C. Everett Koop at the New School University forum "Cigarette Seduction," New York, Feb. 5, 1998.

12. From the Congressional testimony of Robert D. Tollison, "The Treatment of Health Providers Excise Tax," in a statement before the Committee on Finance, April 28, 1994.

13. Kenneth E. Warner, "Employment Implications of Declining Tobacco Product Sales for the Regional Economies of the U.S.," *Journal of the American Medical Association*, April 24, 1996.

14. Author interviews with Gary Black, former tobacco analyst with Sanford C. Bernstein & Associates, and Morgan Stanley tobacco analyst David Adelman.

15. Interview with David Adelman.

16. Interview with David Adelman.

17. Euromonitor PLC, *World Market for Tobacco* (London: Euromonitor PLC, 1997, 2000).

18. Euromonitor.

19. Philip Morris Cos. press release, "Philip Morris Reports 1999 Results," May 26, 2000.

20. Euromonitor.

21. Suein Hwang, "Smokers' Game: Philip Morris Passion to Market Cigarettes Helps it Outsell RJR," *Wall Street Journal*, Oct. 30, 1995.

22. Dow Jones Interactive Company Reports.

23. *Dow Jones Business News*, "B.A.T. Will Buy Smaller Rival Rothmans for $8.67 Billion in Stock," Dow Jones & Co. Inc., Jan. 11, 1999.

24. From R.J. Reynolds press release, "R.J. Reynolds Tobacco Holdings, Inc. Reports 1999 Fourth Quarter And Full Year Results," Jan. 27, 2000.

25. Susan L. Hwang and Paul M. Sherer, "RJR Nabisco to Shed Tobacco Businesses," *Wall Street Journal*, March 19, 1999.

26. Dow Jones Interactive Company Reports.

27. Euromonitor.

28. Colman McCarthy, "Exporters of Cancer," *Washington Post*, July 1, 1989.

29. Euromonitor.

30. Euromonitor.

31. Euromonitor.

32. Laura Zinn, "Marlboro Country Blues: To Get On Its Feet, Philip Morris is Cutting 14,000 Jobs," *Business Week*, Dec. 13, 1993.

33. Euromonitor.

34. Tobacco Institute.

35. Philip J. Hilts, *Smokescreen: The Truth Behind the Tobacco Industry Coverup* (Reading, Mass: Addison-Wesley, 1996).

36. Richard Klein, *Cigarettes Are Sublime* (Durham and London: Duke University Press, 1993), 188.

37. David S. Broder and Dan Balz, "Gore Had to Cross Numbness Barrier On Tobacco Issue; Distance From Sister's Death Led Him to Oppose Smoking," *Washington Post*, Aug. 30, 1996.

38. Tara Parker-Pope, "Major Tobacco Companies Increase Cigarette Prices by Five Cents a Pack," *Wall Street Journal*, May 12, 1998.

39. Robert G. Wyckham, "Regulating the Marketing of Tobacco Products and Controlling Smoking in Canada," *Canadian Journal of Administrative Sciences*, June 1, 1997.

40. Peter Taylor, *The Smoke Ring* (New York: Pantheon Books, 1984).

41. Glenn Frankel, "U.S. Aided Cigarette Firms in Conquests Across Asia: Aggressive Strategy Forced Open Lucrative Markets," *Washington Post*, Nov. 17, 1996

42. Euromonitor.

43. Frankel.

44. Frankel.

45. Frankel.

46. Klein, 188.

47. Anthony Flint, "U.S. Tobacco Goes Global," *Boston Globe*, June 23, 1996.

48. Charles Babington, " 'Exporting Death': Cigarette Firms Attack Asia as Americans Smoke Less," *Los Angeles Times*, July 23, 1989.

49. Tara Parker-Pope, "Smoke Signals: Legal Pressure in U.S. Doesn't Cloud Outlook for BAT Overseas," *Wall Street Journal Europe*, April 2, 1996.

50. James Rupert and Glenn Frankel, "Big Tobacco's Global Reach: In Ex-Soviet Markets, U.S. Brands Took On Role of Capitalist Liberator," *Washington Post*, Nov. 19, 1996.

51. Suein Hwang, "Sucked In: How Philip Morris Got Turkey Hooked on American Tobacco," *Wall Street Journal*, Sept. 11, 1998.

52. Hwang.

53. Rupert and Frankel.

54. Flint.

55. Euromonitor.

56. Author interview with Judith MacKay, March 1996.

CHAPTER THREE

1. Maurice Corina, *Trust in Tobacco: The Story of the Men and the Events that Created the Great Tobacco Companies* (New York: St. Martin's Press, 1975), 48.

2. Tobacco Institute, *Tobacco: Deeply Rooted In America's Heritage* (Washington, D.C.: Tobacco Institute), 10.

3. Tobacco Institute, "Tobacco Industry Profile," 1997.

4. Tobacco Institute, *Tobacco: Deeply Rooted In America's Heritage*, 12.

5. Greg Otolski, "Growing Controversy: A Time of Toil Exacts Toll, Tobacco Harvest is Back-Aching Work With Added Dangers of Poison and Falls," *The Courier-Journal*, Louisville, Kentucky, Aug. 28, 1994.

6. Terri Ballard et al., "Green Tobacco Sickness: Occupational Nicotine Poisoning in Tobacco Workers," *Archives of Environmental Health*, Sept. 19, 1995, p. 384.

7. "Illness Tied to Exposure to Wet Tobacco," *Knoxville News-Sentinal*, Sept. 28, 1994.

8. U.S. Department of Agriculture, "Malawi: Tobacco Annual Situation Report," *USDA Reports*, May 29 1998.

9. John Stackhouse, "Lush Garden Flourished in Drought-Ravaged Country," *The Globe and Mail*, Sept. 28, 1992.

10. Thomas Land, "Poor Countries' Future Going Up In Smoke," *The Globe and Mail*, April 22, 1981.

11. Tafadzwa Matumba-Mumba, "SADC: Food Crop Production Insufficient for Population," *Inter Press Service Global Information Newtwork*, Nov. 12, 1992.

12. Bob Williams, "New World Order: North Carolina Takes a Back Seat as Tobacco Thrives Abroad," *The News & Observer*, Raliegh, N.C., April 9, 1995.

13. Tara Parker-Pope, "Possible Boon for 'Renegades' Becomes Issue in Major Firms' Settlement Talks," *Wall Street Journal*, Nov. 4, 1998.

14. Yumiko Ono, "For Philip Morris, Every Store Is A Battlefield," *Wall Street Journal*, June 29, 1998.

15. Philip J. Hilts, *Smokescreen: The Truth Behind the Tobacco Industry Cover-up* (Reading, Mass.: Addison-Wesley, 1996), 60.

16. Richard Kluger, *Ashes to Ashes: America's Hundred Year Cigarette War, the Public Health, and the Unabashed Triumph of Philip Morris* (New York: Vintage Books, 1997), 422.

17. David Krogh, *Smoking: The Artificial Passion* (Oxford: W. H. Freeman, 1991), 25.

18. Kluger, 6–7.

19. Ruth Sorelle, "Morning's First Puff Has the Right Stuff for Smokers, Report Says," *Houston Chronicle*, Nov. 27, 1997.

20. Hilts, 186.

21. Hilts, 44–45.

22. Claude E. Teague, Jr., "Research Planning Memorandum on the Nature of the Tobacco Business and the Crucial Role of Nicotine Therein," April 14, 1972.

23. Alix M. Freedman, "Impact Booster: Tobacco Firm Shows How Ammonia Spurs Delivery of Nicotine," *Wall Street Journal*, Oct. 18, 1995.

24. Todd Lewan, "Dark Secrets of Tobacco Co. Exposed," *Associated Press*, Sept. 12, 1998.

25. Associated Press, "Firm Uses High-Nicotine Tobacco: Certain B&W Brands Get Altered Leaf," *Richmond Times-Dispatch*, Feb. 11, 1998.

26. Kluger, 746.
27. M.A.H. Russell, "The Smoking Habit and Its Classification," *The Practionier* 212 (1974): 793.
28. Ernest Pepples, "Industry Response to the Cigarette-Health Controversy," 1976.

CHAPTER FOUR

1. Gerard S. Petrone, *Tobacco Advertising: The Great Seduction* (Atglen, Penn.: Schiffer Publishing, 1996), 34.
2. Company annual reports.
3. Claude E. Teague Jr., "Research Planning Memorandum on the Nature of the Tobacco Business and the Crucial Role of Nicotine Therein," April 14, 1972.
4. Jeannine Stein, "Smoke Signals Activists Sound An Alarm About Young Women, Media Images and Tobacco," *Los Angeles Times*, April 27, 1994.
5. Petrone, 7.
6. Joseph C. Robert, *The Story of Tobacco in America* (Chapel Hill: University of North Carolina Press, 1949), 124.
7. Robert, p. 232.
8. Robert, p. 233.
9. United States Department of Agriculture, *Total and Per Capita Manufactured Cigarette Consumption, 1900–1995.* Washington, D.C.: United States Department of Agriculture.
10. RJ Reynolds Tobacco Co. Advertisement, 1938.
11. Morton Mintz, "Cigarette Ads Said Full of 'Health' Cues," *Washington Post*, March 10, 1988.
12. Robert, p. 238.
13. American Tobacco Co. advertisement, 1932.
14. Stuart Ewen, *PR! A Social History of Spin* (New York: Basic Books, 1996), 159–162.
15. Ewen, 165.
16. Ewen, 164–165.
17. John Stauber and Sheldon Rampton, *Toxic Sludge Is Good for You! Lies, Damn Lies and the Public Relations Industry* (Monroe, Maine: Common Courage Press, 1995), 26.
18. Jacob Sullum, *For Your Own Good* (New York: The Free Press, 1998), 36.
19. July 1938 *Reader's Digest* quote cited on www.tobacco.org.

20. USDA. *Total and Per Capita Manufactured Cigarette Consumption, 1900–1995.*

21. Richard Kluger, *Ashes to Ashes: America's Hundred Year Cigarette War, the Public Health, and the Unabashed Triumph of Philip Morris* (New York: Vintage Books, 1997), 151–158.

22. Kluger, 182.

23. 1926 Marlboro Advertisement.

24. Joan Kufrin, *Leo Burnett, Star Reacher* (Chicago: Leo Burnett Co., 1995), 159.

25. Kufrin, 160–161.

26. Kufrin, 162.

27. Kluger, 292.

28. Stanley Cloud and Lynn Olson, *The Murrow Boys: Pioneers on the Front Lines of Broadcast Journalism*, 288.

29. Kluger, 128, 171.

30. Cloud and Olson, 289.

31. Kluger, 327.

32. Kluger, 335.

33. Action on Smoking and Health, "Tobacco Explained," www.ash.org.

34. Stanton Glantz, John Slade, Lisa A. Bero, Peter Hanauer, and Deborah E. Barnes, *The Cigarette Papers* (Berkeley, Calif.: University of California Press, 1998), 258.

35. Glantz et al., 365.

36. Ibid.

37. Sylvester Stallone letter to Bob Kovoloff, dated April 28, 1983.

38. Glantz et al., 370–388.

39. Glantz et al., 367.

40. Glantz et al., 368.

41. Glantz et al., 372–373.

42. Glantz et al., 372.

43. "Smoking in Movies Is Increasing, in Contrast to Real Smoking Rates," *Business Wire*, March 2, 1998.

44. Center for Tobacco-Free Kids.

45. Philip J. Hilts, *Smokescreen: The Truth Behind the Tobacco Industry Cover-up* (Reading, Mass: Addison-Wesley, 1996), 66.

46. Cathryn Jakobson, "Why They Stretched the Slims," *New York Times*, June 8, 1986.

47. Hilts, 69.

48. Hilts, 77.

49. Action on Smoking and Health, "Tobacco Explained," www.ash.org.

50. Ibid.
51. Claude E. Teague, "Research Planning Memorandum on Some Thoughts About New Brands of Cigarettes For the Youth Market," Feb. 2, 1973.
52. RJR memorandum, 1973.
53. RJR marketing presentation, Sept. 30, 1974.
54. Hilts, 95–98.
55. J.P. McMahon memorandum, Jan. 10, 1990.
56. RJR memorandum.
57. Dolores Kong, "Tobacco Ads' Effect On Youth Attacked," *Boston Globe*, Dec. 11, 1991.
58. "The Tobacco Trade: The Search For El Dorado, Tobacco Companies Look For New Markets Outside US and Western Europe," *The Economist*, May, 16, 1992, p. 21.
59. Stuart Elliott, "Advertising: Joe Camel, A Giant in Tobacco Marketing, Is Dead at 23," *New York Times*, July 11, 1997.
60. Tara Parker-Pope, "Tough Tobacco Ad Rules Light Creative Fires," *Wall Street Journal*, Oct. 9, 1998.
61. Federal Trade Commission report to Congress for 1995.
62. Mary Assunta, "Cigarette Companies Prey on Asia's Young," *USA Today*, May 18, 1998. For an extensive discussion of brand stretching and efforts by tobacco companies to circumvent advertising bans see Infact's 1998 report, *Global Aggression: The Case for World Standards and Bold US Action Challenging Philip Morris and RJR Nabisco* (New York: Apex Press, 1998).
63. Carl Scheraga and John E. Calfee, "The Industry Effects of Information and Regulation in the Cigarette Market: 1950–1965," *Journal of Public Policy & Marketing*, Sept. 22, 1996, p. 216.

CHAPTER FIVE

1. World Health Organization, "Fact Sheet No. 154," World Health Organization, May 1998.
2. World Health Organization.
3. World Health Organization.
4. Jerome E. Brooks, *The Library Relating to Tobacco Collected by George Arents* (New York: New York Public Library, 1973), 3–173.
5. Brooks, 3–173.
6. Philip J. Hilts, *Smokescreen: The Truth Behind the Tobacco Industry Cover-up* (Reading, Mass.: Addison-Wesley, 1996), 3.

7. Taft Wireback, "Lorillard Was Warned In '46," *Greensboro News & Record*, Sept. 26, 1992.

8. Doug Campbell, "Lorillard Documents: Revealing Documents Discuss Nicotine Levels and Marketing to Teens," *Greensboro News & Record*, June 28, 1998.

9. Carl Scheraga and John E. Calfee, "The Industry Effects of Information and Regulation in the Cigarette Market: 1950–1965," *Journal of Public Policy & Marketing*, Sept. 22, 1996.

10. USDA.

11. Hill & Knowlton memo, "Background Material on the Cigarette Industry Client," Dec. 15, 1953.

12. Hill & Knowlton memo.

13. Claude Teague, "Survey of Cancer Research With Emphasis Upon Possible Carcinogens from Tobacco," Feb. 2, 1952.

14. Hill & Knowlton memo.

15. Hill & Knowlton memo.

16. For this and other industry documents, see the web site www.tobacco.org.

17. Hilts, 8–11.

18. Hilts, 13.

19. Scheraga and Calfee.

20. Scheraga and Calfee.

21. Peter Pringle, *Cornered: Big Tobacco at the Bar of Justice* (New York: Henry Holt, 1998), 130–131

22. Glantz et al., 109.

23. Action on Smoking and Health, "Tobacco Explained," www.ash.org.

24. Philip Morris memo, "Two Complexes, a Compound and a Campaign," April 23, 1958.

25. Richard Kluger, *Ashes to Ashes: America's Hundred Year Cigarette War, the Public Health, and the Unabashed Triumph of Philip Morris* (New York: Vintage Books, 1997), 325.

26. Kluger, 258–259.

27. Ibid.

28. Ibid.

29. USDA.

30. Centers for Disease Control Office on Smoking and Health, "Smoking Prevalence Among U.S. Adults," July 1996.

31. Kluger, 350–358.

32. David Phelps, "1970 Gallaher Document Could Be the Smoking gun," *Star-Tribune Newspaper of the Twin Cities*, April 12, 1998.

33. Action on Smoking and Health, "Tobacco Explained," www.ash.org.

34. Gene Borio, "Tobacco Timeline," Tobacco BBS web page, www.tobacco.org.

35. Centers for Disease Control Office on Smoking and Health, "Smoking Prevalence Among U.S. Adults," July 1996.

36. Action on Smoking and Health.

37. Ibid.

38. Hilts, ibid.

39. Lionel Van Deerlin, "Koop Was Surprise to Both Sides; He Pulled No Punches," *San Diego Union-Tribune*, July 25, 1989.

40. 1982 Surgeon General's Report.

41. J. L. Charles memo to T. S. Opsdene, "Comments on Future Strategies for the Changing Cigarette," Feb. 23, 1982.

42. Kluger, 617.

43. Euromonitor.

44. Euromonitor.

45. Jeff Cole and Jeffrey Taylor, "Liggett to Cooperate in Tobacco Probe: Pledge by Small Company Is Seen as Turning Point In Move Against Giants," *Wall Street Journal*, April 29, 1998.

46. Suein L. Hwang, "Tobacco Firm Gives Frank Advice Online," *Wall Street Journal*, April 9, 1999.

47. Hilts, 7.

48. Hilts, 26.

49. Jeremy Laurance, "Firms 'Suppressed Safer Cigarettes,'" *The Independent*, March 4, 1999.

50. Ernest Pepples memo, "Industry Response to Cigarette Health Controversy," Feb. 4, 1976.

51. Glantz et al., 117.

52. Various industry documents.

53. John Schwartz, "Reengineering The Cigareette," *Washington Post*, Jan. 31, 1999.

54. Myron Levin, "Trial May Shed Light on Demise of 'Safer' Cigarette," *Los Angeles Times*, Aug. 27, 1998.

55. Laurance.

56. Martin St. Lucie, "Philip Morris Halted Work on Safer Smokes," *Palm Beach Post*, Nov. 25, 1998.

57. Michael J. McCarthy, "RJR's Premier is Off—But Not Running: In Trials, Sales of 'Smokeless' Cigarette Falter, *Wall Street Journal*, Dec. 12, 1988.

58. Alix M. Freedman, " 'De-Nicotined' Next Gets Pitched By Philip Morris Just Like Decaf," *Wall Street Journal*, August 4, 1989.

59. Suein L. Hwang and Alix M. Freedman, "Smokers May Mistake 'Clean' Cigarette for Safe," *Wall Street Journal*, April 30, 1996.

60. Donald P. Baker, "High-Tech Device Makes Smoking Less Smoky," *Washington Post*, Dec. 8, 1998.

61. Suein L. Hwang, "Latest Move to Make a Safer Smoke Uses Special Tobacco," *Wall Street Journal*, April 29, 1999.

62. New School University Forum, "Cigarette Seduction," New York, Feb. 5, 1998.

63. Ruth Sorelle, "Cigarette Tax Increase, Ad Ban Urged," *Houston Chronicle*, Jan. 28, 1989.

64. Tara Parker-Pope, "Danger: Warning Labels May Backfire," *Wall Street Journal*, April 28, 1997.

65. Krogh, 99–114.

66. Ernest Dichter, "Why Do We Smoke Cigarettes," *The Psychology of Everyday Living*, 1947.

67. Krogh, 63–65.

68. Krogh, 44.

69. Krogh, 65–68.

70. Krogh, 54.

71. Tamar Nordenberg, "It's quittin' time; smokers need not rely on willpower alone," *FDA Consumer*, Nov. 21, 1997.

72. Eben Shapiro, "Big Spender Finds a New Place to Spend," *Wall Street Journal*, Oct. 6, 1994.

73. Brooks.

74. Nordenberg.

75. 1980 Surgeon General's Report.

76. Ilene Barth, *The Smoking Life* (Columbus, Miss.: Genesis Press, 1997), 80.

77. Klein, xi.

78. Italo Svevo, *Confessions of Zeno* (New York: Vintage International, 1989), 8–11.

79. World Health Organization.

Chapter Six

1. Jerome E. Brooks, *The Library Relating to Tobacco Collected by George Arents* (New York: New York Public Library, 1937).

2. James I, King of England, "A Counter Blaste to Tobacco" (New York Public Library, Arents Tobacco Collection, 1604).

3. Brooks.

4. Jacob Sullum, *For Your Own Good: The Anti-Smoking Crusade and the Tyranny of Public Health* (New York, The Free Press, 1998), 28–30.

5. Sullum, 32.

6. Richard B. Tennant, *The American Cigarette Industry: A Study in Economic Analysis and Public Policy* (Archon Books, 1971), 135.

7. U.S. Department of Health and Human Services.

8. Richard Kluger, *Ashes to Ashes: America's Hundred Year Cigarette War, the Public Health, and the Unabashed Triumph of Philip Morris* (New York: Vintage Books, 1997), 69.

9. Amy Becker, "Minnesotan Kindled 1st Anti-Smoking Day Idea in '73 Newspaper: Grew Into 'Smokeout,' " *Chicago Tribune*, Nov. 21, 1998.

10. U.S. Department of Health statistics.

11. Memo from J. Michael Jordan, "John Robinson's California Cases," April 29, 1988.

12. Peter Pringle, *Cornered: Big Tobacco at the Bar of Justice* (New York: Henry Holt & Co., 1998), 14–21.

13. Benjamin Weiser, "Tobacco's Trials," *Washington Post*, Dec. 8, 1996.

14. Alix M. Freedman and Suein L. Hwang, "Leaders of the Pact: How Seven Individuals With Diverse Motives Halted Tobacco's Wars," *Wall Street Journal*, July 11, 1997.

15. Weiser.

16. Philip J. Hilts, *Smokescreen: The Truth Behind the Tobacco Industry Cover-up* (Reading, Mass: Addison-Wesley Publishing Co., 1996), 113.

17. Hilts, 114.

18. Weiser.

19. Hilts, 123.

20. Freedman and Hwang.

21. Weiser.

22. Richard Leiby, "Smoking Gun: Merrell Williams, Ex-actor, Is the Most Important Leaker of Documents Since Daniel Ellsberg," *Washington Post*, June 23, 1996.

23. Leiby.

24. Leiby.

25. Max Boot, "Rule of Law: On the Trail of the Cigarette Papers," *Wall Street Journal*, April 10, 1996.

26. Glantz et al., 15.

27. Leiby.

28. Freedman and Hwang.

29. Alix M. Freedman, "The Deposition: Cigarette Defector Says CEO Lied to Congress About View of Nicotine," *Wall Street Journal*, Jan. 26, 1996.

30. Freedman.

31. Suein L. Hwang and Milo Geyelin, "Getting Personal: Brown & Williamson Has 500-Page Dossier Attacking Chief Critic," *Wall Street Journal*, Feb. 1, 1996.

32. Benjamin Weiser, "Tobacco's Trials," *Washington Post*, Dec. 8. 1996.

33. Freedman and Hwang.

34. John Schwartz, "Florida Smoker Wins $750,000 in Damages," *Washington Post*, Aug. 10, 1996.

35. Alix M. Freedman and Suein L. Hwang, "Burning Questions: Tobacco Pact's Limits—and Its Loopholes—Pressage Fierce Debate," *Wall Street Journal*, June 23, 1997.

36. Suein L. Hwang and Milo Geyelin, "Is Tobacco Settlement Good News for Industry?" *Wall Street Journal*, Nov. 17, 1998.

37. Suein L. Hwang and Milo Geyelin, "Tobacco Industry to Rethink Its Defense," *Wall Street Journal*, Feb. 12, 1999.

38. Christopher Buckeley, *Thank You For Smoking* (New York: Random House, 1995), 124–125.

39. Jeffrey Goldberg, "Big Tobacco Won't Quit," *The New York Times Magazine*, June 21, 1998.

40. Milo Geyelin, "Tobacco Lawsuit Filed by Guatemala Dismissed by Judge," *Wall Street Journal*, Dec. 31, 1999.

41. Ernest Beck, "B.A.T. Finds Breaking Up Isn't A Hard Thing To Do," *Wall Street Journal*, Sept. 7, 1998.

42. Michael Connor, "Philip Morris Exec Tells Jurors Marlboro-Maker Changed," Reuters News Service, June 12, 2000.

Index